An Adult's Garden of Verses

From whimsy to "what if" and back again;

(mostly) verse

for light **hearts and** enquiring **minds.**

Joel H. Hinrichs, Jr.

Copyright October 2017 Joel Hinrichs

Words With a Mission   All Rights Reserved

ISBN 978-0-9970326-4-2

DEDICATION

A child knows his mother more intimately than any other person in life, yet at the end there are often surprises. The child's eye forms an image so ingrained it may resemble taking Mom for granted – she is what she is, and as she is, simply because that's *who* she is. The opportunity to see a parent through other eyes too often climaxes at the Final Gathering. So many friends assemble and display a panoply of rich associations, many of which fruited after the nest-emptied adult's children went away to form their own adult selves; this can present a two-edged surprise. Was my parent so complex, so astounding, as that? How wonderful to realize it, and how great the remorse to understand fully just after she is gone. *"Well, dearie, all your mother's friends knew it, and realized what sort of human being she was as early as the days when you were spitting up on her shoulder."* I knew Mom as a quiet being of constant love and strength, but guessed (incorrectly, I suspect) that she was the norm. She was *my* norm.

Mother, the verses and the book are for you, as is the astonished heart that dedicates them to your memory. Reflecting dimly the love I received from you, and more love than I realized I had,

Joel

Ruth Marguerite Arend Hinrichs, in Memoriam

Rest now in peace, beloved Mother, you
Unwont to rest while others had a need;
Though now the trappings of your life are few,
How fewer still have seen your breadth of deed.
Might every soul who knew you think on this,
Against the pull and push of human strife,
Regardless whom one asks, without a miss,
Good Meg had naught but friendship in her life.
Unable are we, still, to sum your parts;
Eternal peace has called you home, we know.
Renewing, loving thoughts fill pensive hearts,
Internal glows that surfaces don't show.
Take now repose with Jesus, Loving Host,
Each moment There your love reflected most.

For Mother; 3 June 1923 – 20 October 2006

INTRODUCTION and ACKNOWLEDGEMENT

Most of these originated on a website called fanstory. If you ever visit fanstory.com, look for a joelh605. That's me, in the bottom right-hand corner of the home page, among the Recognized Reviewers.

Fanstory is a site for those who aspire to an avocation, or in some cases a vocation, in print. The rules there are simple, and the cost of membership is small. Basically, write whatever you want, but observe common courtesy, not just because that's always correct, but also because the audience, like the language, is world-wide.

It works as a "committee-of-the-whole" critique group, where members earn fanstory dollars by critiquing others' work. You use the same currency to buy the incentives that pay others for reviewing your work. Real money also works when buying the incentives. Using real money also makes the site stronger and rewards the guy who runs it.

Each to his own, but for me this is why the site is useful:

a)   Contests – I have not found a better source of ideas to write about than somebody else's pet notion, or photograph, or crazy hoop to jump through (see Captain Stormweather's Journey to Heaven pg **Error! Bookmark not defined.** for one example.)

b)   Variety – There are people writing in English over the world.

c)   Camaraderie – all fanstorians are willing to be your friends. Read their work and tell them honestly (and gently!) what is good about their work, what isn't, and how to fix it.

d)   Rule 1: DO REVIEWS.

e)   Rule 2: Include all three elements (praise, problem, progress.)

This book consists primarily of rhymed verse, and concludes with a personal narrative on the art of writing poetry.

TABLE OF CONTENTS

JoAnn Elizabeth

September 8, 2007; the day Joann and I were married

Switch "Joel" and "Jody" depending on who's reciting that first line. Recite alternating pairs of lines, until each has made the complete vow. Best done by taking lines 1, 2-3, 4-5, etc. opposite lines 1-2, 3-4, 5-6, etc. The wedding guests will hear each line twice, then the next line twice. Each speaker both follows and leads, to show two lives becoming one.

Wedding Vow

I, Joel, take thee, Jody, dearest heart,
To be my spouse, to have, to hold, to woo.
I pledge before our God my every part
Is yours; I share both want and wealth with you.
Our gathered friends can see this joy we share,
But also sorrow, trial, illness, woe,
If they be yours, I take as mine to wear
Until, endured, they vanish as the snow.
You are the wind beneath my wings, my muse,
Best friend, dear blended heart from heaven's mold;
We join our journeys in this place, to cruise
Or carom, toward that sunset, silent, gold.
So on your hand, my dearest love, this ring
Is token of our faith, our everything.

'Fluffy' is a code word for the disheveled way my beloved hands me the newspaper. While the text is an actual apology, the acrostic evens things up a bit. ;-)

Fluffy Wife Jody

For how long have I known thee, mistress wife?
Lament I now that it has been too short.
Uneven though we partner, Mrs. Knife,
Flame singes at my heart when I mis-court.

Forever and a day is faulty time
Your keen and fevered soul to comprehend;
Whenever have I mustered wit sublime
Inough to navigate your curves, to mend?

Far be it from my mind to lose kid gloves,
Especially when yours show signs of wear;
Just shoot me now if pushes comes to shoves
Or any other way I'm hard to bear.

Delight of morning, noon, and every night,
Your humble husband loves with all his might.

Birthday poem for Jody, (*76th: 'trombones old')
(April's Ides give way: April 19th)
All seven dwarfs appear to celebrate my princess, of course in
alpha order.

Snow White Dwarf

So <u>Bashful</u> are we, darling wife? We play
Naive? You're trombones* old, your PhD.
Obliges all to call you <u>Doc</u>, and may
We also contemplate your long CV?
Why downplay this? It's <u>Dopey</u>, Dear, to feign
Hum-drumly mews of discontent when April's
Ides give way. You're <u>Grumpy</u>, oh it's plain,
To break another twelve-month's cruel tape.
Extremely <u>Happy</u>, I recall, a true
Delight from May to March, have flowed the days
Which now come 'round to candle time; yet rue
Again? Grow <u>Sleepy</u> by the candles' blaze!
    Redeem your year, my pollen-<u>Sneezy</u> dove;
    Forever's barely long enough to love!

An opening chapter of my love for JoAnn; spring, 2006

I Walk A Path

I walk a path of shadows, loss and wreck;
My deeds return to haunt me and accuse,
Yet you, my dearest comfort, kiss my neck
And yearn to rumple sheets (yet I refuse).

O awesome sis-boom-buddy girl, good friend,
You stiffen Sergeant Pepper, long asleep.
The light reflected from your heart's both end
And shining start of day, and when I leap

From bed to board to desk and back again,
Each part so light it's like I floated there,
Your sunshine flows within each darkened den
My former life has laid; you break the snare.

And now, beloved Nightingale, you know
That you have healed who may yet be your
beau.

Fifth Anniversary

Because you come to me with more than love,
Because you start each day with baptized smile,
Because with you push never comes to shove,
Because without you life is Elba's isle.

My love for you is human, yet ablaze;
My love for you is softer than a kiss;
My love for you is past all paraphrase;
My love for you is why I live in bliss.

You take my hand and lift my heart above;
You take my heart and give it milky joy.
You take my heart and you, my turtle dove,
You swell it up like Helen come to Troy.

 Five years have come, have gone, and what are we?
 Beloved, all I know is, I love thee.

THOUSAND PETALS

Thou art a rose, and hast a hundred reds,
Hues changing, furl-unfurling, constant grace
O'er all thou touch'st. Thy petals? Watersheds
Unfolding dew on arid hearts, moist lace.

Sit by me, flower bride, and help me soothe
A dryish sense. Enfold my cracking core,
Now balming; waft redolence, pungent, smooth
Distracting mathy Mars, the matador.

Perturb me new each day. Each petal that
Exposes beauty tells the sun to hide
Til you have shown it how to beam, full at
A face that loves you back, unqualified.

Let not these strain-ed sentiments be all;
Such greatness, love, demands one's faithful all.

The first real love poem I wrote for JoAnn; summer, 2006

Burly Moon

The burly moon has whispered down the sky
Through smoky coils of cloud that fracture sight,
While I but wonder at the blight of knowing my
Beloved sees this moon with me tonight
But out of reach of arms that ache to hold
And not in smell of breath or flowered scent,
Nor can I feel the satin sheets unrolled
From sweaty passion, stirred but never spent.
Outside the night has all the parts we name
When lovers hover quiet, each near each,
Yet here my window walls the night, to frame
It glassy as the portrait of my peach,
    My beauty, solace, queen of mystery and pow'r
    Whose love I savor, silent hour on hour.

FanStory challenge: "Consider the moon:" An alternate version.

Yon Diva Moon

Yon diva moon is singing down the sky,
through smoky threads of cloud that tickle sight.
Her song is subtle, deeper than a sigh
and I can't glim the words, try as I might.
Within my inner being, shy and slow,
the moon's grand glowing serenade so bright
awakes a sleepy soul to magic's glow;
it makes a wish that endless be the night.
But only night? The moon's unwasted pow'r
is there within, disturbing sleepy-heart
to dance, to woo, to make a lover's bow'r
and claim his lover, aiming Cupid's dart.
    So does the moon reform the one uncouth?
    Or does it pull the drapes from feelings' truth?

Both of these were for Jody's 77th birthday

Cute Honey Bunny (Jody)

Can any gal of dicing years stay so
Unsanded by the decades' rasp? Has love's
Thesaurus words to capture that? And glow! -
Each glance you send me seems like velvet gloves.
How cute you look, when morning lights the room.
One glance at you, unwashed and painted not,
Necessitates a second; and you bloom,
Each morning like the first. Your smile is hot!
Yet look again, while soap and paint apply;
Before you were my earth, you're now like fire.
Unleash the fleet of Helen! Beautify
No more that regal face, lest I expire!
No doubt about it, Hon, you fill my life,
Yet always I want more, beloved wife.

Seven Come Eleven

Say what, my darling Jo, another year
Expired, and you astride the April page?
Vermillion lips, bedazzling eyes, "Fold here!"
Expressed in sidelong glance, "Come take your
    wage!"
No staple 'cross your tummy, purring wife,
Can mar the smooth perfection I behold.
O'ercycling waves of zest and scholared life
Mix well with hungry kisses, deep and bold.
E'en now at seven times eleven, those
Embracing arms enfold in full 3-D.
Lest I retreat to stare at one flat pose,
Exhume my wand'ring mind to day, and thee.
Veil not the beauty of your being, dove –
ENtrust it to your husband's dumbstruck love. .

For Valentines Day, 2009

My Dearest Love JoAnn

My dearest love JoAnn, my bride, by day

You bring me sun and gladness. Each time I,

Dumbfounded, catch your smile it golds my clay,

Embosses me, rapunzels me so high.

Around you joy is never far or faint;

Rambunctious bunny, how you bounce! If you

Exhibit frowns or any small complaint,

Some tempered coil within turns m'yow to mew.

Today we Valentines renew our troth,

Lay out our love before each other's feet;

Of any pair we've held our wedding oath

Vivacious, solemn, joyful daily treat.

Eternal pledged yet daily forged anew

JOANN, my love, I'm no one without you.

JoAnn Elizabeth

Just seeing you, my springy wife, these eyes
Obey Saint Paul's command: look only at
A thing that's lovely, pure, a blessed prize,
Nuanced at times but always God-begat.
No matter what may come, your inner spring
Exerts a love, a grace, that brushes off
Laments or second thoughts; you always sing
Ignition when my heart goes "Sputter; cough!"
Zvengali are you? Magicker of love?
And then I say, are you an angel sent
By God, a winged guest from high above?
Engage me, sleep within my humble tent.
Take this for certain, Jody, blessed wife;
However short or long, you are my life.

Love Sonnet for Jody

How can I speak the depth of what you mean
To me? How eye your face or form, how trace
My princess' coming to my life? How lean
Was I before you—now I'm fat with grace.
You are so fierce at smiling, quick to bless,
Your presence always joyous, well, almost!
That strength of heart and soul can be a mess
But then abruptly make my frown a ghost.
And what am I that you should love so much?
How pure your wanton hugs, how wide your arms!
I bless the day our friendship turned from "Dutch"
To friendly kiss, then fire, then five alarms.
   We smile our thanks each day at God above;
   Forever isn't long enough to love.

A Crown of Sonnets for JoAnn
I Friendship

You spoke to me before I spoke to you,
and seemed so quietly restrained, genteel,
yet saw a stronger me than ere I knew;
so in-born is your trust – you see in steel.
To my surprise you held a PhD,
and said it was an every-day detail;
how many times you've said, "Just let it be;
we're peers, my friend, I'm not beyond the pale."
Since I was wed and you had loving ties,
no thought of more than buddy-ness arose.
And buddies? yes we were!—I realize
how well we walked the way that friendship grows.
From Bible class, to lunches, so it went;
we even saw a movie once or twice.
Your effervescent inner rosy scent
has made—and makes—your nearness softly nice.
So friends we started out, and friends we are.
You are, my dearest love, my pilot star.

II Sharing

You are, my dearest love, my pilot star.
I steer by you whenever I am out.
Our dif'rent views can clink the cussin' jar
but words blow over; nothing dies but doubt.
You asked me, "Pray with me right now, my girl
is having trouble and I grieve." I took
her gladly under whispered wing. What pearl
of tiny price, a pray'r—then my world shook.
My namesake, youngest child, abandoned life;
you came, you calmed me, helped me learn to grieve.
His mother also ceased to be my wife;
we'd grown apart, she chose her time to leave.
You brought, my wondrous friend, your steely grace
and rosebud kindness, dauntless quiet dawn.
You saw that I was no one's basket case,
but there before my feet was Rubicon.
From sharing grief we turned to sharing joy;
Sweet sis-boom-buddy girl, I'm buddy-boy.

III Talking

Sweet sis-boom-buddy girl, I'm buddy-boy,
your "Little Brother Joe" or LBJ;
the time we spent together ran from coy
to midnight secrets not for light of day.
I knew that you were blue-state, I was red;
While passionate in that, I learned your mind
was open to debate, a watershed—
to meet the enemy, and find her kind.
We found our cognate dissonance a chore
but also knew that difference is right;
no bonding binds friends fast unless its core
sustains a friction; heat plus love makes light!
We talked in time 'bout sex—right after church
while eating lunch we'd calmly retrogress;
our terms could make a nearby diner lurch,
though none e'er stalked away in blue distress.
    I loved those conversations with my Jode;
    you always serve your topics a' la mode.

IV Teasing

You always serve your topics a' la mode,
including those where a' la mode is dill.
Your red-state beau is "LBJ"? You rode
that horse to death—I say he's dead—lie still!
And yet, you never tease, just love too hard;
you're one who can't recall a single joke.
Your sense of humor's like a St. Bernard,
All warmth and wine, and kisses, and a poke.
By contrast I'm a handful, full of fun,
and ready to extract the lighter side
of any little slip, inject a pun
from center field—but (almost) never snide.
One time I sprang from under blankets, roared—
it gave you such a start! You hadn't seen
me there. Your silly grin was like the Horde
of Huns had come to take you for their queen.
    But then, belov'd, you mounted an attack,
    my gorgeous pillow-fight'n demoniac.

V Courting

My gorgeous pillow-fight'n demoniac,
your image fixed fore'er in mental eye,
I courted you in hope of feather-smack—
might call it childish?—I say apple pie!
Sweet Jody, you're a hugger, and I guessed
you slyly meant to hug me en amour.
So did I jump the gun? But I felt blessed
to get a hug that wasn't quite demure.
And then we kissed. That distant boyfriend? Past.
Our stories differ on who felt it first,
but does it matter? Tiny actions cast
our lots; one sip may kindle life-long thirst.
And yet, the struggle we endured, the cost,
missteps, and months we spent apart. Old loves,
allegiances misplaced, smiles gone to frost—
each put or felt a test—we gentle doves!
    That said, we built our house on solid ground.
    Endurance builds respect; we each feel crowned.

VI Marrying

Endurance builds respect; we each feel crowned
in having won the other's hand. We learned
all over how to honor dodgy ground
a partner hallows; lasting trust is earned.
Who gave my love away? Her firstborn, Paul;
Best man? My eldest son, my scholar, Chris.
At our age, history is vast, and all
summed up to just the iceberg's tip of bliss.
A grandma who's a bride must play the mom
and do a mother's duties; all the same
she wholly needs her calm, her mantra "Ommmm"—
too soon she's called to referee the game!
And then she flows serenely down the aisle,
A masterwork perfected over time.
I sing, "You come to me", watch ev'ry smile
go misty—and September's summertime.
    From "single blessedness" and settled ways,
    We joined our lives to share the golden days.

VII Living

We joined our lives to share the golden days—
and find ourselves immersed in change and work.
Those small details, two lives to paraphrase
into a quiet hymn—"Soleil du cirque"!
Two schedules to combine, two habits set
in softer shades of stone; one works a.m.
to supper, one from noon til owls forget.
One garrulous, one still as Bethlehem.
And when we courted, who were they, we ask,
those pals who shared deep secrets in the dark?
Oh, we're still here, it's us behind the mask;
The stretch of time is thinning out the spark.
The steeplechase awaits, and watch us go!
We tag team past the obstacles and wear.
If I should falter, there's my partner Jo;
You're wind beneath my wings, my breath of air.
    And though "I saw you first" this much is true:
    you spoke to me before I spoke to you.

Contemplative

A simple saying on how to approach life.

Object Lesson

One day my mother shed a little light
with heat. She boiled an egg, some coffee beans,
a carrot. "So, my daughter, must you fight
and worry, fret and tire, beyond your means?"

"The carrot falters first; it goes in tough
but soon surrenders, falls, and softened lies.
The egg reverses course; when boiled enough
its shell contains a tough and shiny prize."

"But coffee! Dear, what happened to the beans?
Perhaps a change, a wrinkle or a chip?
They're what they were before! Know what that means?
Pick up the cup, my dear, and have a sip."

"The water changed two things, in nothin' flat,
but coffee changes water – be like that."

Friends, this is a tale of the incessant cruelty that all too often plagues our farms and barnyards; the life of a meat animal is dangerous, cruel, and downright thankless! Herewith a:

<u>Vegan Lament</u>

Imagine you are hearing this sung to the
tune of Ghost Riders in the Sky (Ahem)

Old MacDonald had a farm, I really was a fan,
He ran it very sparingly to a very modest plan.
For one, his pig had just three legs, not four like you or I -
I said, "Tell me the story!" He began with a loving sigh:
E I E I Aaaaay, E I E I OOOooooo
Love that pig, don't ya know.

That wondrous pig done saved my life, not once but two times over;
He snatched me from the Reaper's scythe, I feed him corn and clover.
I pledge to keep that pig alive as long as I am able;
You will never see his flesh upon a stranger's table.
E I E I Aaaaay, E I E I OOOooooo
On four legs did he go!

One day out plowing on a hill in ground all wet and muddy
My tractor made like Jack and Jill—that pig, now he's somebody.
He jumped his pen and ran to me and rooted with his snout,
Dug until he'd set me free and hauled my carcass out.
E I E I Aaaaay, E I E I OOOooooo
On four legs did he go!

Another time twixt dark and dawn my house was showin' smoke;
Once again he jumped his pen and pawed my wall a poke.
I woke right up, had an awful start—that fire didn't happen;
If not for yonder pig so smart, right now I'd be dirt nappin'.
E I E I Aaaaay, E I E I OOOooooo
On three legs does he go!

Mercy sakes, Mac Donald, man, your tale one question begs:
What injury befell that pig to put him on three legs?
He looks at me askance—Mon Frer, you take me for a dunce?
An animal such as that one there, you don't eat him all at once.
E I E I Aaaaay, E I E I OOOooooo
On two legs will he go-ooo-ooo-ooo-ooo

[voice tapering, rising into a wolf's howl]

Imagine a log house on rolling prairie, surrounded by
wheat stubble, long abandoned and its windows black
squares of emptiness, nothing above or beyond it but sky.

Was this a house my father saw

Was this a house my father saw when he,
A young man, rambled through the harvest days?
Did he espy this house through wheat-chaff haze
Like smoke that sky'd the farmer's praise to
Thee?
You see us, Lord; we're looking at the husk
That housed the farmer then; yet he is dust
With all his praise now blown away. And must
Our own day scatter into night? Brief musk
Once called us forth to lust and bear; our young
Who spent our youth have gone away, a smoke
We raise to thee. We die and leave unspoke
Our further praise, these counted days now sung.
   This ruin shows us nows unguessed at then;
   Each new now rises, incense, to Amen.

Philosphical Statement

For God so loved the world that He sent
His only Son, my Lord, to die for me:
Within this frame he gave me, put a bent
To string together words; they tumble free
Yet march obediently across the page
To make what sense He gave me power to find.
What then, when others' sense does not engage
And makes a discord with my finite mind?
Do I then rage against this darkened place
Or rise in consternation to refute?
Look, how my Lord was gentle, speaking peace;
How can I other than to follow suit?
   For list'ning gets more gain than through the ear -
   One's list'ning opens other hearts to hear.

I'd Plant a Tree

What information means the most? What fact
or datum takes first place? Suppose you knew
the green door hid your lady? There intact
you'd walk—bright tiger waits behind the blue!
Or is the faith learned at your mother's knee
the One, the True?—which loving mother's Word
is right, (the others wrong)? You'd like to see
for sure which one is which? (Faith says, "absurd!")
"Suppose I knew today's my last—I'd plant
a tree!"—So said a wise and holy man.
And would you like to know your day? I can't
believe I have the wit, the steel, to plan.
   Far better, then, to live abundantly;
   pretend each day is 'it'- and plant a tree.

Fanstory challenge": discuss envy

Apologia for Envy

It's good to have a reason for your fit,
as long as privacy constrains the scene,
i.e. so no-one sees you flinging spit
or comprehends that, inward, you're just mean.
Content with what you have despite the glare
of next door neighbor's gaudy, flaunted gilt:
or writhing on your floor in dark despair
that you've far less to show of what you've built.
So, Envy, do you move me to exceed
or tear me down in acid turbulence?
Does all your energy increase my deed,
or do you force me down behind my fence?
   I see—it's not you making me do X,
   it's all me, making excellence from hex.

Fanstory challenge: acrostic "home sweet home:

Home Sweet Home

Hardy hellos at the hearth from Hon,
Open arms from moonlight unto sun.
Mother to my children, one by one;
Everything I long for when day's done.
Sweet abode that shelters my beloved,
Wall to wall it knows our ebb and flow,
Even though we sometimes have it rugged.
Earthy, warm in winter, summers shaded,
Ties that bind are knitted here, you know.
Here you have my passing memorandum;
Open up this letter from the heart!
More I search, the more I know I've found 'em -
Every day I long for night to start.

Inspired by a photo of a young woman, 1890's dress, lying akimbo and asleep, in sunlight alongside a small stream.

To Do, or to Dream...

What form lies here, what death of day has shut
these eyes? Is even sleep a blessed gain
'neath flowered bush where sun and shade abut?
Can bosky buzz and scent be cursed pain?
What shadow realm has Waterloo'd the plain
of waking day and overthrown the storm
that living must entail?—what increase feign,
what birth where dream shades life in deathly form?
Yet see this echo in the grass, this corm
where kindred ecstasy and agony
connive; sleep's mental flexure sets a norm
our waking hours can neither hold nor be.
Sleep on, akimbo, princess 'neath the sky,
Wreak high, swing low, do't all right where you lie.

Fanstory challenge: 52 word acrostic, each word tracing the alphabet from z to a and back again.

Determining whether or not this assaults the notion of White Supremacy is an exercise left to the reader.

Z-A-A-Z

Zeke yearned xenophilically;
Weird Vernon's uniracial theme
Suspended rational query 'pon
Our noble meritocracy!
Lesser knights join infantry,
Held 'gainst fearsome enmity:
Defend collective brotherhood!
Albatrosses always bear
Calamity, deny each fair
Geometry; hurl into joust
Kings' liberty, magnanimous
Nobility, obedience,
Patriotic qualities.
Recall sublime temerity;
Upbraid vultures wishing
Xenophobic yucky zeniths.

Fanstory challenge; verse must rhyme on every tenth word, starting with
7th (my choice of where to start, right?) AND must address God to ask
whether the human race should be allowed to continue living on Planet
Earth.

Written in iambic heptameter, abab cdcd .rhyme, except where
overridden by the every tenth word rule

Captain Stormweather's Journey to Heaven
(Greatly Exaggerated)

One night I dreamt in high elation, stepping into realms
Of glory. Angels soared and sang ovation: "One True God
Who owns all praise and all Creation!" There I stood with palms
All clammy, dumb with consternation; yet before I trod

One step I saw, with trepidation, God Almighty there
Before me, looking on with quiet contemplation; "Son",
He said with patient love and smile of invitation, "Tear
Yourself away from all of that and take libation—one

Of my most fav'rite nectars is the sweaty exhalation
Of the stars in—what you call that wat'ry constellation?
Right! El Dipper Grande; Son, you'll like its smooth rotation
On your palate; try a sip and see. What exploration

Brings you here this evening?" "Sire! my protopalimpsest
Of explanation is, I'm dreaming You (urk!) what I mean
(oh, botheration!)—Here I am, Lord, making this request:
My exploration, as You have it, is just that, a lean

Imagination's appetite; I seek." "You seek! Sweet pup,
What stimulating compilation are you looking for?
Or have you found some satiation just in beaming up?"
I'm stunned, disoriented, swirled by agitation, floor

And ceiling swapped. Yet, curious, I stay, my station fixed.
"My Lord, I simply seek." With one-eyed speculation He
Takes stock of me a while: "A cash accumulation? mixed
As that can often be, both robbers and taxation see

More use of cash than thee; or maybe information is
Your 'thing'? Empowered? Wiser? Does your faith need
    inspiration?"
"Exalted Lord, Omnipotent, to do all that is fizz
Sodation, not a thing to break a sweat on, mere notation

Which You may choose to do, or not, nor hesitation at
The choosing." "Still, you seek a gift? What obligation can
You undertake to prove you'll treat it well, relation that
You'll own?" My child? My only son? What palpitation can

My heart endure? "My child, what is your correlation there?
I only want that you return as your donation your
Commitment, voluntarily to safeguard and to care,
Full preservation, for the gift I freely give you." "Sure!"

"One consideration nags, and that's your prior work."
"Sir, on what occasion did I ever once appear
Up here?" "Your current situation? You've never had this perq!
But where've you been?" "Location wise my boyhood home was
    near

A Pittsburgh smelter operation, then I went to Rice;
Since then a fact'ry automation firm has moved me all
Around the West." "Uhuh. Carnations in your yard? They nice?
And do you tend their irrigation? Mulch them in the fall?"

"Who, me? Yeah, my procrastination wasn't good for them
Last year." "Well, Sonny, they're Creation; it's a gift; in fact,
The universe is My imagination, whether phlegm
That guards your nose, your own genetic information, tract

Of land you walk on, wide blue oceans, constellations—do
You get my drift? Child, all without an obligation, none!"
—I was floored. "Dear child, you've put My inspiration through
The mill; it's on your watch that rampant degradation's run

Amok." "Lord, there is no defense; a dread anticipation
Says you may decide to kick us off for depredation!"
"Child, you bathe a babe which poops; the water's despoilation
Is a shock, but which do you discard? Ayyup! Hydration!

Babes we keep, and clean, and guide when their flagration stokes
Our ire." "So then might Earth get new regeneration? Some
Now think we've wrecked the air, the seas, conflation; smoke's
The harbinger of fire! we've raped the earth; invasions come

For oil and ore; we've et the fish; predation is our weft
And theft our souls' loom's warp. Ablation and consumption make
A trail the blind could track." Hilariation glowed from left
To right on's face: "My glad donations! Yes, you've Esau's take,

You eat your Birthright—Jacob's passion when you swipe it, too!

My other presents? Some starvation, for a prod: a slew
Of needs and wants; salvation from your greed? I gave you minds.
Salvation from Damnation? Gave you hearts, and Jesus, too.
All for cause." "Illumination? Can I know what kinds

Of purpose you established?" "Perturbation's mine; some things
You'll never need to know." "Again! Illumination, Sir!
Among us there are those who rape earth's lamination! Springs
Of water flung on rows of hills, wet mastication fer

A trinket!" "Child, I loved it! Power's transformation both
Of order and of chaos, each from each; causations feed
On change. There's gold, you found it. Exaltation!" "Sir, I'm loath
To see in you a joyed destruction." "Boy, take up and read

My Jewish Scripture; lad, that inspiration can be read
As the orig'nal owner's guide. Want indication re
Chaos? Kings One nineteen 'leven: ' *The LORD said:*
Station yourself upon the mountain; God will in '(that's Me)'

Perambulation pass you by. A mighty wind broke rock then:
Creation's master was not there; and then an earthquake but:
Creation's master was not there; and then a fire: again
Creation's master was not there. And then a quiet 'Tut!':

Creation's master whispered. Child, I Am that tiny voice,
Prophetic consumation. Did you marvel at the Quake,
The Wind, the Conflagration? Child, I built the All by choice,
My Word's Cogeneration, dense enough that it would take

Ten thousand human generations just to pull the m
From e, so c's squaration could be known. Your greatest minds
And scholars in cooperation have begun to glim
The outlines of The Bang; imagination ope's the blinds

For them to number it, but limitation of the human
Form (and mark the tiny decades' annuation since
Your theories escaped those older, easier to glom-on
Prestidigitations) mortal form will make a mince,

Can only grope conceptualization of a fact,
Or large or small. Your bestest imitation seems to be
The like of tiny sons whose emulations, strutting, act
Out Daddy's role in Daddy's shoes, his ideation: 'Me

The daddy now! I showing how!' What fond elation lifts
Your heart to see him so?" "That awesome elevation takes
Me far away from self! My boy's proud adulation gifts
My life in measure past mere words or calculation, makes

This old heart young!" "And also Me. Your graduation, cat,
From ignorance to growing understanding of My World's
Initiation makes me proud." "But are you worried that
The discombobulation we've unceasingly unfurled's

Getting out of hand; it's Your Creation!" "Humor me,
My child; it's only Earth, and any cultivation falls
To you, for good or ill. It's yours! Expatiation on
These blights is wonderful, but you are not plantation thralls.

Your stewardship perturbs me. Notwithstanding that, in your
Origination you will find a flake of Me—your minds?
Remediation takes both mind and heart; you've both, and more!
Speciation's track, My hidden Hand, bequeathed you kinds

Of grit, evasion and reaction skills you're going to need
To 'scape obliteration; here's the rub: before I let
You leave Play Station Earth, you'll have to get it right, and bleed
Fixation Green, clean up your act. Diplomacy will get

The nations started; all reliefs must happen first before
I open exploration's door. Arrange your sandbox, Child.
The treehouse beckons; my congratulation then will pour
permission to bestride its floor!" God gratiation smiled.

Fanstory challenge: use four supplied phrases (bolded) to say something coherent. This is a 'Dear Joan' letter, and _not_ to my beloved JoAnn.

Fantasy on Four Phrases

With what **unspoken promise** did you ask
To be my future, honor hope and dream?
What wink or wrinkle did you use to mask
Your empty loom—no woof or warp, no beam

Or even yarn? Damn any grin that **shielded**
The pain beneath your dark eye, ever dimmer.
You prose where poetry is life, unyielded
Breath from scanty depth. No **sparkles glimmer**

There where honesty is knife and spoon
To cut the meat and lift the food of love
To lips that pout **the lowest point**, balloon
In sighs and catch the salt from eyes above

    That fill in love yet overflow in hate
    For you, pretender, needy, never mate.

What would yours be?

My Three Wishes

Mistakes are made to be corrected, so
you'd have to wonder, should I cancel mine?
To think my acts would have such power? No,
have faith, I'll not fix either mine or thine—
regard the altruistic side of life;
evolving social problems just abound—
eliminating war, crime, hunger, strife?
What genius can wrap three wishes 'round
immensities like those? So what can one
see fit to do? And should you look that gift
horse in the mouth? Whatever wrong you shun,
eliminating problems doesn't shift
so much as undercut the race we've run.

The speculation was borrowed from another, but the verse is mine.

Speculation (other's)

I sail across the deep to edge of sky
and ride the subtle tides to understand
how death can chase my sun and moon from high
yet leave the stars to guide my eye to land.
Within tall gates, across an ancient bridge,
abandon mist and water, enter trance;
a childlike, curious desire, a smidge
of fear—I hearken to a dark romance
where one by one the puzzle pieces drop,
disclose a difference, both conquer sense
and help us learn that death is life's great crop
where all our gain falls due as recompense.
    A Life past life would matter not, unknown;
    yet in this trance I trust, where trust was sown.

Spring

We've carried coats, been harried by cold snow,
Endured slick ice and slush, and drafty bow'rs
Down which we walk, through barren trees to go
Where buds will someday bloom, become bright
　flow'rs

Which scent the air, aroma therapy
With pow'rs that bring the heart to life, to learn
From scent that green can grow again, can be,
Can rise from battered leaves. Unfurling fern

And rising crocus, lily, rose, each tells
Us that the season's cycled; lather's gone
To rinse, and then to spin, soon heat compels
The perfume, and becomes the summer's dawn.

　　So endless ages run from bud to rust
　　And back; but spring's the one that gloats, "I
　　　LUST!"

Fanstory Challenge: Use at least *nine of ten* specific *words*
    (all ten are present [highlighted])
    (and in alphabetic order)
    (and the sonnet is an acrostic)

Under all these constraints, there is no guarantee that its content
will be intuitively obvious to the casual reader ;-)

Flower or Titan; What's Your Will?

November is the month the weather **bleeds**
Its warmth away; a whale has **blubber** that
No **cold** can breach, but weather's dewy beads
Expire on Jack Frost's breath, their **death** low-fat.
O heavy **fate**, your foot on blubber's back,
Fine **formula**s send men against the whale
To wound its **head**, to stop its **heart**, to crack
Each breast, for oil to make a black night pale.
Not so the weather, back ashore; its hand
Works hard to shape each season's course. To **risk**
Oneself against its strength will quickly land
Remorseful folk in illness' arms: "Too brisk!"
Define yourself then, make no compromise—
Supine, as **rose** to wind, or whale that dies?

This was written from a picture. Do the barn wall, the sturdy, X-timbered Dutch door, the berry bush beside it, and the afternoon sunshine arrive intact in the mind's eye?

Old Oaken Door

Dear oaken door, gone gray with age—unyielding
Beams like folded arms denying entry, shielding
What's within.

Those holly berries on the bush say summer's
Done, its fire is damped, and autumn whispers
Quiet, thin.

Old door, time rasps your hinges, frame and pane
Alike both fired by sun and lashed by rain,
Yet standing guard between Within, Without; plain,
Solid, Dutch.

A double door, you're latched above, below:
Perhaps a horse had home behind you? Know we
Just this much,

That what's within is mute, but prized, has shelter,
Only out when needed—tack, some seed or fodder,
Tools, and just

Like you, in being homely, rough, and strong:
And proud, organic, passing, here for long
And yet to dust.

I praise you, Door, (and please forgive the rocks
I'd throw against you after Dad would box
My ears) old Door!

Whimsy

The More we Make

The more we make that greenhouse gas,
The faster will the icebergs pass.
The more those shining icecaps shrink,
The more our beach-fronts face the drink.
So if you want to stave off worry,
Just don't drive in such a hurry!
Burma Shave

Anaximander's Ragtime Band
(Z to A)

Zooey's yellow xylophone,
William's virile undertone,
Thumbelina's saxophone,
Rory's quiet piccolo,
Obadiah's nasophone,
Michael's limberlipped kazoo,
Jamming incandescent heights,
Getting funky every day,
Crazy, banging, AY!

Little Red Riding Hood
(the True Story)

There was a happy country girl whose name
was Li'l Red Riding Hood; she'd been "Giselle"
before but every day that very same
red wrap was there; she loved it all too well.
Now little Red lived in a house that sat
upon the forest edge; and mother's mom,
her granny dear, lived through the forest at
the marge of pastures green, near Handsome Tom.
Since Granny wasn't feeling well our Red
was up for taking her a jug of soup,
and cookies too, so she could eat in bed.
"Don't spill," said Mom, "Or all you'll have is goop!"
"And while you're being circumspect, beware
of what's within the wood; odd dangers lurk
for those who are not careful, dear—a bear
could wear you on his face, as just a smirk!"
"Yes, mother dear, I know the drill," said Red
with quietude; she donned her hood and walked
outside, but not into the wood; instead
she carved a whistle from a willow stalk.
Its sound was oh, so fierce! Our Red was cool,
she knew that lots of men were in the wood
to cut the trees with axe and saw. No fool
was Red—she'd whistle loud—they'd help their
   'Hood.
So Red strode in, along the path, when what
to her surprise, a hairy form beside
her stood, and spoke to her; he sounded phat
but wore no clothes; all she could see was hide.
"Ahem," he said, "Dear Riding Hood, perchance
you've got a goal? You look all bizness, that's

for sure—I'd love to walk 'longside." "No pants!"
was all she said—that nearly drove her bats.
"Tut tut, my dear, that's how we are, these parts
are hard to shop in." "'K," she said, "you ac'
polite; I'm off to granny's. See, her heart's
not good these days; I'm taking her a snack.
Sir, you seem nice, but in these woods they say
both wolves and bears abound. My granny's crib
is up the path, but I'd look sharp—no way
to tell when you'll find trouble, rib to rib!"
"Dear girl," said he, what is your name?" "I'm Red,"
said she, "And what is yours?" "I'm Cainous
    Lowbow,"
answered he, then left, nay almost fled—
so ghostly, though, she couldn't hear him go.
"How odd was that?" she asked herself, then went
upon her way. She crossed a meadow bright
with blossoms, picked a few, inhaled their scent,
then back to woodsy shade, as dark as night.
Her granny's door stood half ajar; she knocked
and entered in; there in the bed she saw
a shape that looked uncommon large. It blocked
the light, but Granny's cap was o'er that maw!
Red crept a step, and said aloud, "Those Ears!"
"I hear you well, my dear!" "Those eyes, so large!"
"I see you too, sweet girl!" "Those teeth -" her fears
were rampant now—her whistle blew the charge.
The wolf leapt up, but that shrill noise was more
than he could stand (those ears, eh?) "OW!" he
    howled,
and fell, a blanket-tangle on the floor.
She got Gran's skillet from the range, and fouled
that hairy beast a time or ten; Red smote
him on the skull 'til he was dead. She quit

the noise then, too, sat down to breathe, took note
of her surroundings, paused to rest a bit.
It made her peckish, and she got a cookie
from the bag. The soup was spilled, but what
was that? She'd turned the wolf to something ooky.
Getting up, she mopped the messy spot.
Just then the doorway filled with men, Big Tom
from next door first among'em; Granny'd gone
for nitroglycerin, now showed alarm
at such a mess! "Dear Red, what did you spawn
"Here in my kitchen? Yes that mop is good,
and thanks for nothin! Spilled my soup, my snack
done et, and dragged that filthy beast in! 'Hood,
you owe me! Clean it up dear, crack your back!
Well, handsome Tom drug off the wolf, and tanned
that furry hide. He made another hood
for Red, much warmer than the other, and
he asked her, "Be my bride?" Then Gran was good
because her Red was cool, you know, the place
was clean, more cookies brought, enough to give
a wedding! Tom the groom had studly grace,
and ever after happy did they live!

The End

Interpolated from table chat at a dinner with two of Jody's lady friends, one of them Ginger. Jim Doe isn't the fellow's real name.

Jim Doe's Misstep

Jim Doe was Ginger's sorta-beau, a guy
In second gear, his 'vroom' putt-putt.
Mistaking Ginger for a god-on-high,
Dear Jim felt trepidation in his gut.
One day a long dead flame relit his life—
Exactly how the 'dead' part 'scaped his gaze
'Scaped Jimbo's brain as well—so Mack the
    knife
Made mincemeat of a courtship of, six? days.
In jig time Jim's old flame extinguished him,
So back he goes to Ginger, full of grief;
Spelunking in a cave of woe recrim,
The hapless Jim defers yet seeks relief.
E'en so it goes with widows, Ginger feels—
Prospective mates, in short? no souls, all heels.

For cat lovers and nephews everywhere. This early attempt at (assault on) the sonnet misses on a couple of technical points, to say nothing of the sort of content one brings to the form

How to Deliver Saddest News

Whilst traveling in Istanbul, I got
A wire from Uncle Ned, who'd kept my cat.
"Puss darted from the curb; a greasy spot
Upon the street shows where she ended at."

"Oh Ned!" I sent as my reply, "How kind
Was that? Far better break the news by small
Degree! First, tell me that she climbed behind

Your back and sits upon the roof. When all
Of that's absorbed then wire again to say
She fell, was hurt, malingers, may not live
To see the morrow. Then at last betray
My tender hopes. When I am ready give

    The awful news." He wired again, aloof,
    "Your nana, nephew, sits upon the roof."

Jody and I role-play via alter egos Billy-Bob and Betty Sue. This
is a letter Billy-Bob writes to his city cousin, with a few
glimpses into our supposed sense of humor. Originally an entry
in a company summer fun time and so-called talent show.

Letter From My Cousin Billy-Bob

I got a letter from my cousin Billy
Bob today; he always has an in-
teresting take on things. He's deep; no silly
talk of war or peace or oil from him.
Uh uh – he's looking out for life the way
a possum grubs for crawdads in the creek.
He met a wonder gal the other day
and soon they'll have been married for a week.
Dear Joe, he writes, My Betty Sue has shore
the greatest way of sizing up a man. She saw
me bending over at the hardware store
and grabbed me, said, "There oughta be a law!"
Now how the heck was I supposed to know
That my durn butt was like a beauty show?

She said, "Oh dearie, you're one hunky guy.
Who sees the gut? You're slim and strong indeed.
Your funny smile, that twinkle in the eye,
's enough to make a woman want to breed."
I looked at her askance – we're old, y'know,
an' asked her what she meant by that? "My dear,
you're bashful, but I think you're not that slow."
That woman's wink is music to the ear.
I gotta say, I thought the world was fine
the way it was; but single life was chips
and beer compared to porterhouse and wine
now Betty Sue has brung her wigglin' hips.
I'd never knowed just what I mighta missed
if Betty Sue din't see my butt; I' blissed!

One day I asked her why she walked behind;
"Dear girl, I like to hold yer hand, and chat."
"Why Billy Bob, you didn't know? Now mind,
A woman wants to keep her eye on that.
"On what?" I asked – I'd never given thought
to what a woman saw from second place.
"Dear Lord, my child, you didn't know your butt
looks so darn hot? – it's cuter than your face."
"You wound me, Betty Sue, but I don't care,
a man is s'posed to be a homely cuss.
But lookin' at my blessed derriere?
I'm 60, not16; I missed that bus."
No tellin what a woman's gonna say;
That Betty Sue's my gal; she makes my day.

She's also good in bedddd-ddding plants and soils.
Ah ha! Y' thought I's going somewhere kinky?
Betty Sue's a farmin girl; she spoils
to dig and weed and work until she's stinky.
A While ago we'uz clearin out some bush
and Betty Sue hauled barrow loads of trash
to dump out back; it's pretty hard to push
a barrow full of sticks and dirt and mash.
Next day she said her arm was awful sore,
and would I take her to the gym; but all
that did was make her shoulder worse – she'd tore
the ol rotator cuff, from large to small.
No tellin' what more we'd'a done, but see,
my woman's health means ever'thin to me!

She convalesced a while – poor weepy thing,
her hair and makeup in a sorry state –
her good right arm all trussed up in a sling,
and Bozo Billy Bob says "You look great!"
At last to cheer her up I reassured
ol' Betty she was still my turtle dove;
"Dear girl, don't linger so, I need you cured!
I've got a dozen barrows out there, love!"
Twarn't long and she was up and makin' song;
she brought me jelly from Kentucky. It
was in a tube and tasted sorta strong -
why boast "KY" on stuff that's so unfit?
Now Betty, she just stared at my durn bread;
"It has another use," was all she said.

Well once she clued me in on what it was,
the kitchen warn't its home no more. I ran
it outta there – Whoooowee! – because
a man should always buy the better plan.
T'other day I tole her she was just
the greatest lookin girl I'd ever knowed.
But she was in a diff'rent place, and lust
was what she heard, not love: "Oh, what a load!"
Just then a spider stood behind my rear,
and barked distinctly, if you take my drift.
"I didn't mean it quite that way, my dear!"
But Betty Sue just laughed and laughed; "A gift!
You put a twinkle in my eye, Sir Bill;
I'll love you more each blessed day, I will!"

Dear Cousin, come and visit us a while.
We never lack fer things ta do; we slop
the hogs, an nut the steers, an dig a pile
a' fire ants out, and make the rattlers hop
from out the ditches; clean the horses' water
trough – you know that you can lead a horse
to water, but you can't persuade him, "Oughter
drop no turds therein?" They've no remorse.
We know our neighbors' bizness, Cuz, and they
fer sure know ours. In twenty, thirty years
you'd start to look like us; why, Cuz, we may
fergit you was a Yankee – hold those tears!!
The life 'round here is easy to afford,
and diff'rent ev'ry day. We're never bored.

Fanstory challenge: write a poem about a strange device, in 200 **words** or less. I think this is 198.

Horace Winkerfoom and his Helibroom

My buddy, Horace Winkerfoom,
Was working on his HeliBroom
When, out the corner of my eye,
I thought I saw a wrinkled guy
About a half a meter high,
With tapping foot and face like doom.

"Say, Horace! You see that?" I cried.
"You got a feller set to ride
Yer doggone broom? He looks to me
Like some Godzilla wanna-be,
All attitude, a synergy
Of witches' brew and lizard hide."

Now, Horace, he's nobody's fool,
He glares at me but keeps his cool,
And lightly, like I'd made a joke,
He says, "Ye've met the kindly bloke
Who's bought my latest master stroke,
The Warlock Junior Travel Tool!"

A greeny grin took shorty's face,
And I have never seen a place
With less to recommend it than
That gritty fellow's furrowed pan;
However small, this tiny man
Could frighten half the human race.

"Well, Horace," says I nice and slow,
"Just how fast does that dingus go?"
The warlock leapt upon the seat:
"A test, and I'll be back to eat
Your firstborn if it don't complete..."
When SNAP he was a fading glow,

And Horace, cool as ice, avowed,
"That snapping sound was much too loud."

Last class of the day (Latin) Spring 1960 – sophomore year of high school. Hearing this at home, Dad thought it was grandly funny; Mom cringed.

The Hummingbird.

I went a-shooting with my gun and shot it off into
 the air.
The little bullet fell to earth in shaded wood, or
 meadow fair.
Perchanced I on a humming bird, singing
 Greensleeves in a tree.
"Say, O tiny hummingbird, won't you sing a song
 for me?"
Then the little hummingbird, dripping tiny drops
 of blood,
told me what he thought of me and fell down
 softly where I stood.

Later I showed it to a friend who was on the school newspaper staff. Raising brevity to a virtue, he shortened it to this:

I fired my gun and hit a bird;
its dying breath was a dirty word.

He was a sophomore, too; can you remember back that far, boys and girls? ☺

Family and Friends

Overstated, but true in spirit. I am so proud of my sister

Proud of You, Peggy

My sister made a cork board for our mom
With corks extracted from her chardonnay,
From vintners Gallo, Mill Creek, Vin de l'Homme,
Their best chianti, zinfandel, tokay.

She kept this up for years, would not allow
Self-sight into her straitened life, her waste
Of talent, cash, efficiency - of how
Her nightly bottle had about erased

Her prospects, health, resiliency, her game.
Besides which Peggy was a smoker, too.
Then all at once she woke up; she became
Twelve stepper, both to booze and smoking! Few

 Are ever strong enough to dare so much,
 Yet you, brave Peggy, doubled in the clutch!

Chris's then-beloved Sandra commissioned this acrostic.

Cute Honey Bunny (Chris)

Cute isn't quite your style, my son, but then
Until you learned to walk that's all you was;
The cutest son I'd ever had, a ten -
Ebullient, happy grinning baby fuzz.
Howbeit, you're all grown, a hairy guy
Of thirty years, a scholar and a gent.
Now comes new decade number four, and I
Extend my wish that it be succulent.
Your darling Sandra thinks you're very cute,
But 'tween us guys we know you're manly stuff -
Unless, that is—remember, you're astute -
'Ntentionally you'll soften just enough.
No son of mine ignores his love's good cheer;
You *are* cute, honey bunny—have a beer!

A lark – co-worker Randy Hilton had a birthday. Note how the acrostic misses juuuuusssst slightly ☺

Randolph Hilton

Regardless whom you ask at EchoStar
And even if you ask Sir Ergen, Chuck,
Da best dang disk drive guy, or near or far
Now stands our guard; he'll never pass the buck.
Our Randy Hilton, sage and always strong
Leaves naught to chance, does everything with care;
Patrolling trouble's ranks, he strides along
Heroic like, bestowing good will everywhere.
His pony tail is sure to cheer us up;
In ways both large and small he smiles at life.
Low times or high, he'll always lift the cup
To every challenge, smile like Mack the Knife.
o Randy, here's to you my techie friend,
Now happy birthday – you're the living end.

Harry Brown passed away a few years ago, age 96, a friend for half a century. His name is 16 letters, thus his 'sonnet' has two closing couplets. How fitting to 'double down' on a truly great human being.

Harry Wesley Brown

How great Thou art, almighty sovereign Lord,
Against the foggy breath of time, when each
Rehearses forfeit, that a love shall ford
Rude Rubicon of death, and leave our reach.
Ye angels cry for joy at sinners' grace -
We mortals grieve our temporary loss.
Eternal Lord, Your smile rewards the race,
Sustaining all who lift their cross across.
Loss brings us on, and yet to celebrate
Ebullient heart, kind soul, most trusted friend;
You, Harry, model wisdom, calm but great,
Beset by age, yet joy is at your end.
Release your spirit, warrior, husband, Dad,
Obey God's last command: go to Him, glad.
Who are you now? Whose master, or whose lad?
Nebraskan once, now Heaven's child, Light clad.

Alanna Kathleen Brown. PhD.
Beloved muse, and Harry's daughter.

Alanna's 73rd

Spectacular and wonderful is how
Exemplar lives are lived, so does my flame
Verboten, yea five decades past, allow
External notice, so august, yet game?

Ne'er mind the gulf, my mickle twinkled past,
Tell only this, that as you've lived, your heart
Yet runs in rain and shouts a vivre amassed
Through grit, and wit, and everlasting art.

Howbeit I, long tranced by thee, should love
Regardless that we never got to pair,
Elaborating histories where 'shove'
Extinguished 'put', unringed, yet ever there.

Your humble and obedient servant, I
Rejoice to see that life still lights your eye.

The sentiment here is taken from Tex-Rozelle Brown;
mother to Alanna, beloved to Harry.

Five Letters to Six

Human
beings aspire
to heights of excellence
yet do not vet their standards with
their peers: "human" is so self-absorbed. That
pinnacle, so simple and so
difficult? You add an
'e' to become
humane.

For Ellen Fiero, whose memory in Nepal holds
mountains, children, wildness, beauty, and Namaste.

OUR DAYS IN NEPAL

Our days in mountain air, the heights, the wind,
Unwinding views of clouds with rocks that high—
Regale you now I will, full fishy-finned,
Delirious tales of hiking in the sky.
Amid the people there, the smiling children,
Yelling, running, leaping, happy boys
So civilized and yet so wild they build
Immutable, the bond of rock to joys.
No taste is universal, but for me
No place has any way to top Nepal.
Enduring in my mind and heart, I see
Perfection? No, but holds me still in thrall.
Abiding peace exists where life is hard;
Lay down your ease; it leaves deep joy debarred.

Sarah Barber has performed in various Colorado Springs operas and other classical music events.

Sarah Barber, Mezzosoprano

Slutty parts that use your form, or vestal
Altar servant, virgin martyr; span these
Roles from height to depth, from earthy pestle
All the way to mortar, pounded on to squeeze
Heroic measure through stiff upper lip,
But yet to giggle slyly with a wink
At every Baron's beck or workman's quip.
Rehearsals 'til all spirits flag and sink,
By pluck you turn your work until it's play!
Everted soul unguarded and unforced,
Resplendent whether castle or cafe,
Meant modesty keeps "haughty" all unhorsed.
Extremes this freighty often fracture those less
Zealous to be simple; thee I bless!

Martile is a diva extraordinaire, and the muse/soul of opera in Colorado Springs, Colorado. (Side note: the first acrostic sonnet I ever did; sort of a "challenge the crisis moment." For good or ill, Martile, you sharpened that first pen.)

Martile Rowland

Most magnificent of mien, O muse
And mentor, teaching youth but also those
Reclining now in graying years, excuse
This modest note, less poetry than prose—
Intending only to address your grace,
Lese majesty, who from a homespun soul
Evolved into superlatives that space
Regrets it can't contain. What other role
Or function could you take to better serve
We plebes, aspirants, lesser fowl and cattle,
Late admirers, those without the nerve
And preparation needed to do battle?
No matter what the may have, could have been,
Dear diva, also thank we James of men.

Don Jenkins headed the Colorado Springs Chorale for over a third of a century, and is, with Martile Rowland, the muse/soul of vocal music in Colorado Springs, Colorado. Dan accompanied, Jackie admin'd, and the last line quotes from just two of the countless choral works Don has directed.

Donald P. Jenkins

Director extraordinaire, your choir
Obeys—it's almost there! Each phrase, each fillip,
Now a snowflake, now a roaring fire;
Attend to diction, every tiny r-flip!
Leaving nought to chance, you draw a map
Detailing every consonant and vowel,
Praying that we learn it and, mayhap,
Jam well enough to silence Simon Cowell.
Expert o'er a span of decades four,
None yet can guess how you and Dan and Jackie
Keep it all together—and, what's more,
Instill in us the highest art, by cracky!
Now here's to you, Don Jenkins, long our chief:
Sing wassail, O Fortuna, you're the beef!

Joel Henry Hinrichs III
In Memoriam

An elegy, in blank verse.

It was in summer, your age two-plus years;
you saw me mow the lawn and held the bag
so I could dump the fresh-cut grass. You knew
so much so soon, and left us just the same
as that, too soon.
            Your brothers told at your
memorial how youngest brother Joe
outfoxed their daddy's bedtime check; he ran
a string from door to light switch, so when I
peeked in to catch them reading after lights-
out, it was dark! They loved you - just how many
youngest sons can have that honor. But
so lonely when they left - your brightness
    somehow
all alone in soul, in dark devoid
of ties and kin; you left your dad and mom
behind and went away. Your spring, a young
man's zest and hope, unwound until you
    drooped,
despaired.
        It was dramatic, even so;
the coroner's report was busy, dull
but cruel, How'd I die me? let me count
the ways - the height and breadth and depth of it
-
yet when I looked upon your flesh that one
last time, your legs and feet looked primed to
    jump,
to rise and walk beside me one more time.

It was October, your age twenty-one.
Your final email seemed so normal, so
quotidian, so day to day; and when
the plain clothes men asked leave to go inside
the house and chat with me, and when I knew
I now was short one son, I did not think
it could be you.
　　　　　　　　We started losing touch
when you were six or so. I took your older
brothers on the road, and mom took care
of Sis, and Joey; then when I came back
you'd shelled in fat, and hoarded food, and not
forgiven me for leaving you behind.
By small degrees we failed to understand
each other, you and I; and though my son
was tall and lean at leaving-time, that shell
was there to hold him in, and keep things out
that mounted higher than his father knew.

It is December, your age marked in stone.
Your trials now are done, your body ash.
My heart remembers both the good and bad
and wishes, ev'ry day, to have you back;
by steps not taken or commenced, I can't.

Ordowahl the Huge and Ugly, 2008

Fanstory challenge: use the sonnet form to write a saga (2008).
Take One: The original suite of poems.

Ordowahl's Journey Begins

Behear ye now of Ordowahl of box-boned face.
Below a waning moon his mother birthed
him. 'Neath a darkened star he gained his place,
Prince Ordowahl the stout, ne'er overgirthed.
Yet straight and strong he grew; while featured ill
his inward parts bore honor's holy flame.
Ninth son, though first in wit, and arms, and will,
he went from Nordish lands to seek his fame.
The king his father sent him, thus: "Erase
yourself from all my realm, for doubt I all
your brothers' love for one with half your grace.
Bestride some other earth; there let fate fall."
   The naming-day that saw him counted man
   was thus the day his legend quest began.

He Comes to Tharcajh

Across far lands rode Ordowahl; his squire
wan conversation kept. O'er years he grew
but larger still, his armor, nay entire
array fell wanting, and he oft got new.
Thus splendid in fresh shining steel, great sword
held high in greeting, Ordowahl appeared
before Tharcajh's gate: "All hail Prince Ord!"
the herald cried, "He'll singe the monster's beard!"
Tall Ordowahl was famed and feared; their need
of him was dire, the monster fierce. Ord came
with stories widely told, a knight whose deed
was deadly, but yet honest, free from blame.
 "Good knight," the king besought him, "Tarry here,
 you'll find this place engaging, I'm sincere."

He Learns of the Beast

The grateful king, Gerfeuil[*] by name, broke fast
with Ordowahl next morn: "Dread knight, we own
a challenge here, you may have heard—the vast
beast Hrunchleir raids us, eating flesh and bone.
We're soon extinct, if none can slay him. Yet
if you, huge knight of box-jawed countenance,
if you of great renown, subscribe our bet,
and save us, here's my daughter's affiance."
Great pity moved the heart of Ordowahl,
as much as any need for wife; he took
no note of dalliance nor bride. Nay, all
his mind was pitched to war, the rest forsook.
 Thus Ordowahl the single-minded knight
 set out to kill the beast in fatal fight.

[*] "gair FWILL"

There is Battle

With all delib'rate haste the prince and squire
went straight to where the beast last fed. "Good page,
but climb this tallest tree, and look for sign of fire
or death. We'll find the beast, then him engage."
Half up the tree the trembling squire o'erheard
a deeper voice than any ere: "You, knight,
shall die! Your metal, flimsy as a bird,
is naught before my teeth and appetite."
From twenty feet, through leafy sighing boughs,
the squire looked down on horse-high Hrunchleir's back,
in time to see stout Ordowahl arouse
the dragon's temper more, with sharp attack.
   The beast, though quick, could never catch his prey;
   anon, a bleeding dragon fled the fray.

The Monster's Dying Curse

My prince," the squire said, scrambling down, "Yon
  beast
has surely gone to lair, to stanch his wounds."
"E'en so, good squire," said Ordowahl, "At least
he'll eat no more 'round here for many moons."
Together then they traced the bloody spoor
past ruined town and village, till at last
they found him, heaped. He muttered something dour:
"My parent, pig, will come and bind you fast."
The beast then died, but with a final cry;
he sent a message, pressed into a squeal
that shivered all the sunny morning sky.
Though wordless, still it made their blood congeal.
   Both squire and prince believed the dragon's curse;
   they knew his parent's wrath would be the worse.

The Curse Unfolds

With pounding heart but steady hand the worn
and blood-flecked Ord removed his armor; while
he slept, his squire restored its sheen. "Adorn
your heart with peace," he said on waking. "Smile!"
They traced their journey back to greet Gerfeuil,
but on arriving what was at the gate?
An angry mob beset them, hurling swill
and fouler garbage, yelling scorn, nay, hate.
There at the head was King Gerfeuil himself;
beside him stood a huge and hearty knight.
Between them Hrunchleir's head lay on a shelf;
the glaring knight wore armor crimson bright.
   With dawning understanding then, they saw:
   dead Hrunchleir's parent stood there, magic, raw.

He Gives a Pledge

"Foul liars, get you gone! You get no wife!"
With sneers and heavy insult as their pay
for killing what had killed Tharcajh's life,
the prince and squire withdrew; 'twas close of day.
Not far from there a weeping sound arose
from underneath a hedge beside the path;
they found a lumpy crone in muddy clothes.
"I'm lost," said she, "'Tis dusk; I fear night's wrath."
Her size was near to matching Ordowahl's
but still she looked so helpless and forlorn,
they pitied her, 'mid her repeated calls
for aid, to keep her safe until the morn.
   "My squire, I cannot tell her, 'Nay'; t'would be
   a sin, and yet – I crave True Sight to see."

His Pledge Redoubled

The squire and prince abandoned pride and made
a lean-to, 'gainst the chill of night. They dug
a fire pit, gathered goodly wood, and laid
a fire, then ate, and made the lady snug.
"Good sirs, your promise please: inspect my state
and pledge to guard me through the dark of night.
I fear some harm, and need your honest rate -
what fee will get me safe to morning's light?"
"Kind woman," said the prince, *if so you be*,
"I'll watch the fire, to keep you warm, and guard
you 'gainst what harm may come. Fear naught from me,
and none's the cost; your watching isn't hard."
　　So through the night, though weary from the day
　　the prince's gaze ne'er strayed from where she lay.

The Monster Wakens

Now, as for Hrunchleir's dam, she fell asleep
and, magic-less, her scaly shape returned.
She knew that honest Ordowahl would keep
his word: she slumbered: he kept watch, and churned.
Prince Ordowahl's one aim was quietude;
she mustn't wake before the break of day
lest she attack while he, in servitude
to honor, make no parry, thrust, or play.
Dawn's ray fell on her monster face; with that
she sprang on him with claw and tooth bared wide.
The prince was weary, sore, and stiff, but hat
was all she got; his sword swept out, split hide.
　　Both monsters—magic, huge and lacking rules,
　　fell prey to Ordowahl's more honest tools.

The Monster's Corpse

The squire had slept but fitfully that night,
and shame-faced asked the prince his health; "I'm here,"
the prince replied, "But do we have the right
to sit and eat, and treat her like small beer?"
"No, Sir," the squire admitted, "We must track
her til she's dead." The prince just smiled, and ate
a bite of supper scraps, and yawned. "My back
could use a bed—but might she have a mate?"
So in due haste, e'er cautious yet with speed,
they broke their camp, and girded up, and went
along her spoor. She hadn't stopped to bleed -
it mattered not, her belly had been rent.
　　They saved the head but burned the meat, and slept.
　　Tomorrow's date with Tharcajh would be kept.

Return to Tharcajh

The smoky pyre of Hrunchleir's dam had cast
its pall across Tharcahj's afternoon.
Next morn the prince and squire awoke; smoke's last
dank tendrils died away, and none too soon.
They moved their camp to water, bathed, and ate,
then turned again to fetch the grisly head.
'Fore noon they stood before the Tharcajh gate:
"Pray tell us, where that reddish knight has fled."
Such question failed to draw a bold reply -
"Good sir, the knight was gone before we knew.
For all we know, your Honors—may we die! -
he moved so fast, it was as though he flew."
　　The people all were shamed, and all knew why;
　　they'd seen and smelt the monster, on their sky.

Demanding a Verdict

Anon the king stepped out to greet the knight,
sat down; beside him sat a queen. Before
them came a girl, with face concealed from sight.
"This was my daughter," said the king; "No more.
She's kin to what you see of me and her,"
he meant the queen, "And shares our type of face."
Gerfeuil was featured ill from wear, and scar,
and blood: his queen made ugly look like grace.
"This head is one day fresher than the first;
we feel obliged to tell the tale entire.
Both Hrunchleir and his dam have done their worst,
and died; you yester saw her funeral pyre.
  So judge us, king, say Good or else say ill:
  what e'er the verdict, be it as you will."

The Verdict Given

The squire stood calm beside his Prince; the sun
was hot that summer's day. The king, in shade,
was loath to give his pledge, his hand, to one
he'd scorned so late. "I'm faint!" then pled the maid.
This roused the king to choosing; either way
he'd play the dunce, but he could read the truth
before him—two dead beasts, one prince. *So pay
the piper, man!* he thought, then smiled. "Forsooth!
You speak about the truth, my knight; hear this!
My daughter, she whose blood sits on this throne,
has power to divine all truth—amiss,
that is, except to fam'ly, blood and bone.
  She's useless to me as a royal guide;
  now take this worthless girl to be your bride."

A Proposition

The girl then said, with voice surpassing sweet,
"Good knight, no matter what my look, your bride -
if e'er I be so—has a star-sign suite
as God ne'er gives without its pointed side.
My natal stars are bright—a full moon too;
I've faith that how you choose can only work
to good." Then spoke the king again, "You woo
this girl or, hear me well, you'll die. Don't shirk!
The wedding or beheading, take your pick,
falls right at sunset. If you see the morn,
she'll judge you, aye, not I; I know she's quick
to tell. Prove true, or fertilize our corn."
  "I fear no death but this: the death of truth.
  I'll wed your miss," said Ord, "or die a youth."

Becomes a Proposal

The prince went on to tell his squire, "My heart
perceives that in this shrouded form there is
no guile or malice, only good. The part
I cannot see is moot—e'en if she's his.
I'm ugly, yet I've friends, and none complain.
Be she alike as homely as her kin,
'tis naught; brief beauty falls away in main
from all the truer traits, one's soul within.
Sweet maid!" he called out, "Come to wife. My hand
takes yours, and we shall go through life as God
ordains; Christ died for us, with no demand
save that we humbly leave pride's ground untrod.
  Gerfeuil, my father soon to be, scaled head
  seems poor compense for her, the prize I'll wed."

From Plea to Vow

"No insult will I hear in frankest speech
from one who's slain a brace of murd'ring beast.
Advance, young Ordowahl. Now daughter, reach
to take the hand that you'll soon judge. To feast!"
Gerfeuil then rose, his queen beside him too;
the crowd there gathered parted as they passed.
The prince, and squire, and princess 'tween the two
kept pace and went along, through crowd amassed.
Though lacking time to fix more tempting fare
the cooks prepared a festive evening meal.
The city folk, it seemed entire, were there
and sang the pair a noisy wedding peal.
  From dragon smoke at morning unto now
  Prince Ordowahl had gone from plea to vow.

Ordowahl Weds

In time the pair were stood before a priest.
Forgoing banns because of King's command
they plighted troth, were bound, there at the feast;
both said the words and ringed a spouse's hand.
The couple then, to hooting catcall cries,
retired unto their first night's marriage bed.
They touched no dinner in the hall; the prize
of joining lives was in their hearts, instead.
The castle seemed to shake with merriment,
yet they heard nothing, none uncandled saw.
Disrobing there with none to help, her tent
flew off as though she'd made fresh air a law.
  So man and wife, unseeing, learned by touch
  who was it that would come to mean so much.

A Wedding Night

"My tender bride, you've made a fearful leap;
how can you join your life, your fate, to one
you've never seen, nor come to know? How sleep
you now, then go live 'neath a diff'rent sun?"
"Please, Ordowahl, if I may use your name,
I know you more than e'en you might have guessed.
Eternal husband, you with heavy frame,
lie down on me; your body's weight is blest."
He marveled at her frank and fearless way,
her trust and free command of him, her lord.
"You have my name. If we together lay,
rehearse me yours; say't now, and prove accord."
   "'Tis Janalei, my husband; need we talk?
   Tomorrow I must look unfit to walk."

Sleepless in Tharcajh

Though huge and used to roughest life, the prince
was gentler than his Janalei could guess;
their coupling was as tender as intense,
and all too soon she lost her maidenness.
"My husband, we've the night entire; sleep not
with me unless you're not asleep." Her wit
made Ordowahl suppress a laugh—it got
a giggle out of bearded cheek. He bit.
"Yes, darling, tell me what you have in mind,
I'm sure we'll stay awake a while." That said,
he started, slower, strong but always kind;
they learned first lessons how to love in bed.
   Anon they found an end to their desire,
   Inviting its return, like dampened fire.

Midnight Conversation

The prince could not conclude his day with sleep
until he knew his bride by more than flesh.
He shook her, even though she slumbered deep,
to straighten thoughts that made a netty mesh.
"My lord, I serve you, and I know your wish;
recall the gift my natal stars bestowed.
Your big-boned face is truly not delish,
and you are sure my own looks like a toad.
I care no whit for beauty, save of heart.
The acts one chooses and one's inner truth
are everything to me; no other part
of you impresses me—not even youth."
　The saucy Janalei thus answered all,
　and snored beside a wakeful Ordowahl.

First Light of Morning

Both first asleep and first awake, she left
to let her maids repair her touseled state.
He glimpsed her going out, her carriage deft;
He also rose, washed, dressed, then pondered fate.
When Janalei returned she took his hand;
"Dear miss," he told the lovely girl, "'Tis good
you've come—I cannot find my wife. Command
me to her place, for all I saw was hood."
"But close your eyes, my lord, and you'll soon see
just who it is has come to start your day."
She stood on's feet then, tippy-toe, made free
to kiss him full; "I'm she, Sir, if you may."
　Prince Ordowahl's red face and slackened jaw
　displayed his heart, undone by what he saw.

The Day Begins

A gentle cough outside their chamber door
betrayed the chamberlain, who'd come to lead
the couple to the royals' rooms. Before
they asked he answered: "Breakfast, if you've need."
Both Ordowahl and Janalei were quick.
She nearly moved the chamberlain aside,
so hungry was her man (she knew)—yet sick
foreboding for her father's ugly side.
The morning after any drunken feast
was taxing on his aging head; his care
to curb an inner rage which never ceased
would vanish when it hurt to comb his hair.
    The prince was hungry, dazzled, and confused;
    his princess was alert, and not amused.

Daring Another Monster

"Come Janalei, tell what you've learned." The king
then gestured to an armored guard, whose flick
of wrist brought sword to ready. "Girl, that ring
upon your finger gives you truth; be quick!"
"Dread father, he whose lineage has been mine,
I'm given, gone, and Nordish. This, my prince,
my Ordowahl, my life, I'll ne'er resign,
nor answer give you. Last night's oath, and since,"
unblushing then she fondled husband's flank,
"Both lead me thus: I'll ne'er debase my kin
by honoring a question quite so rank."
The king's displeasure rose; his lips grew thin.
    "I've ever closed the day of one who'd dare
    to cross me, which you've done. Your deaths seem fair."

A Contest of Swords

Then Janalei addressed the guard: "You, Will:
we played as children on the village green.
You've now your job to do, for good or ill.
Do yours, as I've done mine; kill Nordish queen."
Poor Will the swordsman's simple grasp of fact
was overthrown an instant, and he sagged,
But kingly nod beside him made him act;
he swung a level sword—one blow, both tagged.
At least, Will thought 'twas so, but Ordowahl
had seen it all before, and stepping 'round
his bride he caught two wrists in's fist; withal
the sword flew up, and stuck—a hollow sound.
　　"The pow'r of death and life may be yours, king,
　　but I am royal, too; shall my sword sing?"

Here Comes the Judge

The sword fell back from carv-ed ceiling and,
hilt first, splashed tureened eggy mess upon
the king. One hand scraped food from face, one hand
went fishing for the sword, hangover gone.
He grasped the eggy sword, and stood. He looked
on's daughter, woman now. Another clan
was hers, and she was theirs. Long anger hooked
him deep, and held him to his deathly plan.
The princess whispered then in spousal ear;
Prince Ordowahl smiled at the king, and said,
"My sire, the head of state is coming here;
methinks her word will stand yours on its head."
　　The king swung round, and calmly through the door
　　a queen most fair strolled in, and held the floor.

The True Queen Arrives

"Well, daughter, son, and Gerfeuil, consort drear;
you're boring us, you know—this farce is done.
Fake queen, Gerfroglienne, just go from here.
I'm back, and see you've all been having fun."
Young Will reached 'round king/consort's shoulder then,
and got his sword back, much the worse for wear,
and Will, Gerfeuil and 'Frog skulked out like men
most badly thrashed, and looking for repair.
"Last kiss for you, my Janalei, this day;
all women weep at weddings for they take
their best belov'd, their daughters, far away.
My prince, beast slayer, love her for my sake.
   I knew the beast was dire, and fetched a band
   of men—to find you, owning Janni's hand."

Unfolding the Deception

"I hurried home as soon as news arrived
that you, dear Ordowahl, had killed the thing
that took so many souls. And HE connived
to purge his hate, pretending he was king!
Dear girl, your aunt Gerfroglienne as queen?
My son, you've stood a test severe to think
that she had birthed the face you took, unseen,
to wed. And, now! Your future's on the brink.
You've no idea, son, the wretched place
one reaches when one's spouse's inner ire
can ne'er subside because he's second place.
My castle's shrunk, but peaceful, less your sire;
   sweet Janalei, outlive this ugly mess,
   your knowledge shifted now to happiness."

A Private Goodbye

"Alas, the duties of a head of state
can leave but little time for one's own wants.
Right now is such a time—my quar'lsome mate,
damn'd consort, soon inhabits other haunts.
My dears, I beg you come again, and bring
a lonely grandma babes to coo and spoil.
Now go. My mother's hand once wore that ring,
you know, Prince; see it safe to your own soil."
A quiet kiss; the princess hugged the queen,
spilt tears from cheek to cheek, then slowly went.
He kissed her too, but on the hand. "I mean
to honor Janalei, my queen, she's heaven sent."
    The prince and princess left a mother's sighs
    to go in search of their own by-and-bys.

Six Wagons

The hallway opened on an inner yard
where six large wagons stood, with goods high laid.
The squire was there, and trying very hard
to look un-smug, in comp'ny of a maid.
Four other couples, maid and coachman each,
appeared; six pairs climbed up to start their trip.
The queen came out and gave a formal speech
as head of state, to bless new partnership.
"Prince Ordowahl, dear Janalei, take leave
now on your journey north; my blessing know
its way to you always. And though I grieve
a loss, Tharcajh has kept her life; now go.
    A life seems long until you feel it bend;
    through you Tharcajh's life escaped its end."

Formal Parting

The queen went to the place where Janalei
and Ordowahl were perched. She asked them both
to drop their heads to her. "Now, while I may,
dear children, Nordish kin, I bless thy troth.
Tharcajhi scepter bless thee, head and hem,
be't known to all that Tharcajh owes you much."
Her scepter gently moved, caressing them;
they raised up, quiet, from the royal touch.
Prince Ordowahl stepped high atop the load
to publish Nordish blessings to the queen.
"Dear mother, Tharcajh ally, your abode
be bless-ed; may your future e'er be green.
   We came a vagabond unto this place;
    receiving much, we give you our lives' grace."

The Journey Begins

The column turned, the gates were flung apart.
Six weeping women sent back waves and cheers
until they passed from sight. With muddled heart
the prince looked at his bride; she felt his fears.
A drying smile rebuffed his gloomy gaze.
"Dear spouse, I've knowledge you'll ne'er ken. Your life
will go from here to yon, as through a maze,
but e'er you'll be my spouse, and I your wife.
Come, Nordish lands! We've much to do when there,
including settle ugly fam'ly fights.
Your kin (so many!) have a certain flair
for that; but you shall set it all to rights.
   Dear Ordowahl, my life, my man, now take
    me home—it's mine now, too. There's much at stake."

This is Take Two (2015), a novel and part 1 of a series of books.
These poems are extracted from the novel; they occur as Prelude,
as Interludes between the chapters, and a postlude

Ordowahl the Huge and Ugly, Book I

Prelude

I sing of Ordowahl of box-boned face
In time of absent moon his mother birthed
him; 'neath a darkened star began life's chase,
Prince Ordowahl the huge, ne'er overgirthed.
What omen hails the homely prince's start?
What failure was it, brought a king to heel?
What sons whose selfish errors slew his heart?
What hope to make monarch's soul anneal?
Come with me now to see the hero's birth,
a mother-nurtured, tutored life unfurl.
See test on test to shape and prove his worth –
From crawling babe to manhood, honor's pearl.
　　What started with an infant's outraged squall
　　began a quest to know, then master all.

Hidden Skies

Three mothers bore nine sons, but not until
this last did one appear with kingship's mark.
Full straight and strong he grew. Tho' featured ill
his countenance was home to humor's arc.
From early on his purposed, patient way,
his study, caught his father's wond'ring eye.
An hour spent to learn a rabbit's way
laid bedrock for his mind to multiply.
A four-year-old who had a policy:
by six his mother taught him that a king
must have a lion's heart, but gentle as a flea;
to fear somebody's size was lessening.
  What promise of a penetrating mind?
  what portent, one of fearless strength, yet kind?

Learning and Conflict

A son who has no mother learns to hate
the one who has but cannot share his dam;
and Magnhild was loath to spend her fate,
her soul, on sons in conflict with her lamb.
His mother's love made Ordo's spirits sing,
and father's stiff-jawed lessons rooted deep.
Adored by queen and manly for the king,
The baby brother never learned to weep.
When out of house, they fought their foe as one;
But in the house, that brothers' glow went out;
A mother's love, Pa's kindly benison,
Made naïve ninth, mum's pet, grow oaken stout.
  So though he started last and had no guard,
  and softer heart, e'en so his will grew hard.

Frowning

A troubled Ordowahl sits down beside
his auntie. "Why so glum?' she says, but Ord
replies, "Should I discuss my manly side?
No issues may I own save anger, joy and sword.
"Instead," he asks, "Why failed you, Auntie El,
to share your own beleaguered soul with me?"
"Because, my pet, you would have good and well
done harm to him who loved a girl like me."
"But if you must, dear Elspet, here's the meat:
all girls are sweet until I speak, and then
they pout, and run away on frowny feet."
"Because you ask for wit from what's a hen.
  "A maid sees she's unfit, and you're the cur.
  Take from me now this thong, my sorrow's spur."

Breaking into Prime

  "My Ordie, please don't fall, lest tending to
your injuries I kneel and stain my dress!"
Ord smiles at Ruta's jest and asks anew,
"Who wrestles here, this trampled plot to bless?"
Smith Vronken had the size last year, but length
has gone to Ordo in the nonce. "Young Prince,
let age and guile tie knots in youth and strength."
But when it's done, it's smith who wears the wince.
The village lasses come to give a kiss;
"You've won this right!" They all line up and smile.
"Just so," says Ord, "I'll hug and kiss each miss
that's here; My gift! Line up in single file.
  They grew fair frank, and Ruta brought a friend;
  sweet laughing shrieks brought matters to an end.

Coming of Age

Though homely, Ord was calm and always kind.
Aside from brothers, all he knew were friends.
His wink and wit made "grumpy" undefined
where'er he went, no matter what his ends.
Which, word or weapon, held his greatest skill?
Outdoing elder brothers brought him strife.
Ninth son, though first in wit, and arms, and will,
he went away to find, and keep, his life.
The king his father sent him, thus: "Erase
yourself from Nordland realm, for doubt I all
your brothers' love for one with half your grace.
Bestride some other place; there let fate fall."
　　The feasting-day that saw him counted man
　　begot the day his legend quest began.

A Journey Begins

Priest Ewald shrove the prince and gave him grace.
"My son, before you go we'll say the Mass.
Now say it with me; 'tis not out of place
for one who's taught his tutor, class by class.
Old Heorald the mage found Ordowahl
whilst he was packing Hammerfoot and mule.
"Young prince, go lean and wary, yet withal
here's meager gold. Spend little! That's the rule.
With parting gift of twenty coins, his horse
And pack mule loaded, Ordowahl went south.
The kingdom's love bedewed him. His remorse?
Eight brothers' hate was arid, like a drouth.
　　A jackdaw eyed his progress down the road;
　　Each peasant's friendly wave made light his load.

Mehrwal

First cousin Mehrwal welcomed him; "I'm glad
to see you, cousin, be a guest. I hear
your father's sent you forth; you're just a lad
and need some space, some air, some female cheer.
"Come plow a field", an elbow in the ribs –
"I've sev'ral lasses waiting for your oats.
Next spring I'll see which woman got first dibs;"
a brisk young widow cornered all his votes.
A week of martial arts and hunting stags
put Ordowahl in better state of mind.
Rough manly humor shared, and manly brags
erased the pall of kinfolk left behind.
  Another set of sad goodbyes; but all,
  this time, gave grace and smiles to Ordowahl.

Vlowohl

A nose-full of brass pennies and a single
silver coin got Ordowahl the royal
quarters at the inn. Past there the king
must use the forest, for the road went coy.
He came to Vlowohl, cousin once removed.
Another hunt, this time with less success;
another round of manly jests disproved
his sense of kinfolk judging him the less.
Host Kleywehl cautioned him to be discreet.
"No household's happy when its serving maids
wax jealous. Son, if pressed, you must retreat" –
The lot of them sang nightly serenades.
  Almighty, was I wrong? Your gift of Eve
  exceeds – how can I thank and not receive?

Kleywehl

The way grew steep, but Ordo thought it brief.
He found the lofty valley 'neath the pass
to Viking lands, and Kleywehl's tiny fief.
"Come, Prince! Be welcome – help us raise a glass!"
Because they were so few the social ties
were close. "My Prince, I'm loyal through the worst,
but will withhold my love if you make prize
of maidens here; they all have beaus who'd burst.
It was a final time to speak at length
of purpose, right and wrong, and noble grace.
What chose twixt high and low? Each had a strength
that served the realm, yet some were high, some base.
  The priest, and she of vi'let eyes, they each
  were loath that he should travel past their reach.

Viking Folk

Toward a rocky pass, up icy steeps,
to find a pagan hut and trampled lea,
a pond, a stream that trickles, grows and keeps
descending 'til a river meets the sea.
The first to see him ran at full attack,
but when he showed his strength and peace they smiled,
passed time in idle chat. From maniac
to slumber, then to parting unbeguiled.
A pagan folk they were, and all who met
him spoke a murky tongue. No nobles bid
him "Hail". But jackdaws lurked, who would not let
the people speak aloud, with mind unhid.
  From lonely ice and rock to river's mouth,
  Prince Ordowahl observed, and traveled south.

At the City Gates

Why block the gate, midafternoons? Why hurl
a rock when travelers approach? Rude speech
and taunts draw doom: a princely charge, a twirl
of body, bludgeon'd, done: as asked, to each.
A jackdaw maelstrom swarms the prince: the ground
accumulates chopped poultry for a stew.
Retreating birds then burble out a sound
like speech. A sneaking arm yanks guard from view.
Anon the gates swing wide, and comes the king.
His royal guard, a scruffy lot at best,
approach and take their spots, a tiny ring
with king at center, Ord and mounts compressed.
   "Art come from Nordland, friend? I'm pleased. Be thee
   a guest; partake my hospitality."

To Joust

"Young Ordowahl, you see we like to joust.
There's time this afternoon to make a run
or two. Poor rudiment'ry skills, hot-housed
like winter flowers beg you, be their sun."
Forsooth, their gear was poor at best. A stack
of this, a pile of that – and halfway 'long
the track a smooth-swept tidy spot, a lack
of hoof prints in the dirt – it all looked wrong.
"Now, Hammerfoot, be nimble; jump that spot
which comes where lances meet. We'll see what sort
of jousters Vikings might become, and not
invade the pit they've hidden 'just for sport.'"
   Ten up, ten down, the last one tipped with steel:
   An oddish drink for prize, with pagan meal.

To Dream

Ord's head was muddled, weapons gone and Saeth's
bird-slimey sword was also lost. He prayed
and fell in bed; he dreamed as though his death's
approaching dirge was tuned, the pyre laid.
It was a duel with the pagan king,
a fairytale of trolls and bridges crossed
by merry goats – a riddle, with a string
attached – to take the soul of him who lost.
The distant voice of Heorald gave Ord
a fleeting clue. The king spit curses at
the mage, who vanished, but Ord's verbal sword
riposted, made the king a democrat.
　　At dawn king Ingvik spoke his royal mind:
　　"We sail at ebb, and can't leave you behind."

Across the Deep

Wet wood may bob in ripples on a lake
but Ordowahl had never seen a ship,
this Viking way of crossing seas. *Now take
your wits to this,* he thought, *no time to slip!*
'Twas huge yet light and strong. Three longboats slid
across the waves. Tide, sail and oar soon made
the land a blur. He stood erect amid
the heaving waves – his gut went waste, betrayed.
Ord called on lessons of the mage, observed
their speed and course. Where lay the sun? Pin's shade
on floating disk to tell its height? Uncurved
they trekked the sea, their track a wet parade.
　　At dusk they lashed their ships for king and claque
　　to set a plan for landing, and attack.

Dry Land

Half-dozen Vikings guard the boats; the pack
makes stealthy trot along the beach. His word
his bond makes Ord stand guard while they ransack
a town. Yet faith is watchful, undeterred.
Cajoling them he wins a wrestling match,
then two. Half-dozen Vikings, stiff and sore,
relax around the breakfast fire. A snatch
of conversation, hold a knife – make war!
A slice, a sudden leap, and all at once
the six are five, and one by one they fall.
Three left with swords – what acrobatic stunts
will get a knife through that? Ord slays them all.
   Intently Ordowahl plucks lives like weeds;
   in prayer he turns to Father God, and pleads.

Flaming Town

With Hammerfoot he drags each sailing ship
ashore; with coals he sets them all alight.
He slices packing bonds to re-equip –
retrieving arms, he gallops t'ward the fight.
Debris and bodies mark the way to town;
afoot in narrow alleys, roofs ablaze,
he meets a band of archers drawing down
and taking aim. The prince's spirits raise.
On Hammerfoot he races 'round the square,
his sword a blur of motion, rage unchaste.
So fast the horse, it seems he's everywhere;
the archers and the knight are laying waste.
   The Viking chief 1King Ingvik makes his peace;
   'mid buzzing flies and rot he seeks release.

After the Battle

Broad daylight stares in disbelief at what
blind acts of war can make man do to man.
Receding smoke discloses war as slut
whose rounded heels pull down whoe'er she can.
A shuddered agony relieved by sleep;
rebuilding starts the moment sun brings day.
Dark daylong carnage takes a toll so deep –
a lifetime's moisture can't unbake burned clay.
A sermon urges thanks as Christians' yoke;
a man named Klarenz cared for horse and mule,
and brought them both to Ordowahl, and spoke
good Nordic; Ewald's brags became a rule.
   The chaos that sprang up, the carnage, plus
   the calm, the jumbled lives? God's calculus.

Taking Klarenz

As all things living tend to do, the folk
began to heal and then repair. Their foes
began to knead themselves to town, shape oak
to oak, take Christ for Odin, recompose.
A partial summer passed in homely deeds,
to tutor pagan souls, rebuild, repair.
Replacing scant possessions soon succeeds;
ere winter comes guests must go otherwhere.
Both Ordowhal and Klarenz, single men,
each found the other good for spending time.
There seemed no skill that Klarenz didn't ken:
but stealing hearts? He was the paradigm.
   So Ordowahl took Klarenz as his fief;
   "Your debt is mine: no longer live a thief."

Homecoming

Despite their loss a horse was worth the gain
of getting Klarenz out of town. The prince
and bondman journeyed south through soft terrain
t'ward bondman's home, tho mem'ry made him wince.
His ease with women was alike his curse;
what magic is there in a woman's glance?
He had a magic too, although averse
to joy; it shaped a lonely dervish dance.
They found the city, and he asked to hide
in Ordo's shade. He told of how he'd been
abducted in the dark of night, inside
a barrel, cheating death but full of phlegm.
   Surprise! The city fathers saw them come.
   What now for Klarenz? Just his martyrdom.

Vinegar

Escorted through the town with pomp and pride,
Prince Ordowahl held lead in mixed parade,
with Klarenz in a trap, and terrified.
Herr Prince advances; bondman? Be afraid!
With suave and courteous speech that left no room
for doubt, Prince Euwart IV described the twist
of fate that might have meant an ugly doom:
Young Klarenz wooed from far too high a list.
His fate had been to prove the faultiness
of her whose troth and dowry brought her there,
new mother to a child with none to bless
it save a goose-cooked chef, one starved for air.
   Poor Klarenz, he of love-forced lonely life,
   had nearly placed his liege beneath the knife.

Game

Poor Klarenz lies in foetid dungeon stark.
To gain his freedom Ordowahl suggests
a bout, but Euwart coldly deems it dark
to risk his vengeance on such costly tests.
"A match of verse? And how undo a rank
offense with flaccid words? A childish game?"
"Yet, Euwart, ponder Klarenz rhyming frank
and powered ode of praise; 'twill bring acclaim.
"And if your town selects among its best:
let him and Klarenz parry words, then choose
between my man and yours. If scoundrel pressed
can praise the highest? Good – if not, I lose."
   Prince Euwart held his guest in odd regard,
   but soon announced a contest for a bard.

Clean

To get his man in wholesome frame of mind
Ord asks the prince to have him sprung and cleaned.
" 'Tis done already – I am not the kind
to leave him chained; he's low but not demeaned.
But your parole is key. He cannot dark
my town until the day he wages words;
I'll not have Klarenz dancing in the park
while his life's worth is lower than a turd's."
We find him shaven, washed, but much the worse
for wear. Prince Ordowahl instructs him how
he'll win his life, by raising laud in verse
to Hammaborg. "Your jokes? I disallow!"
   So Klarenz, soul of jibe and merry wit,
   must win reprieve by rhyming counterfeit.

Verse

"O Hammaborg," the poet sang, and won
the city's wreath. "Old master Fridoric!"
poor Klarenz cries – "The man who'd jettison
his cook, in barrel dumped into a creek!"
"Yet what if I should win; will he repay
my debt of pain and death? Will he be flayed
in center square if mine's the better lay?"
"Fear not, my bondman, do not be dismayed."
So Euwart's children pick ten simple terms
that Fridoric and Klarenz both must use.
On view in public square each poet squirms
in fevered thought, while praying to his muse.
   Anon the songs are sung, and one is fine,
   but Klarenz writes the purer, higher line.

Ironworks

The fragile Klarenz needed many'a kink
worked out of cramped and idled limbs. His kind
liege lord restored through sweat the bondman's pink
of health – could Klarenz say "I'm disinclined?"
Yet good Frau Schlach, who'd scribed the old frau's hymn,
was also grandma'd by his aimless smirk.
The rich girl's father was Herr Schlach, quite grim,
but owner of a thriving ironwork.
So when the prince has asked the worthy Herr
a favor small as this, to hire the wretch,
he nods assent, then shoos Ord out of there.
Yet one more craft; for Klarenz it's no stretch.
   Day passes day the winter long, while Ord
   trains Klarenz more, who also trains his lord.

Social Graces

The lady Rigomonde made a plan
to groom the foreign prince for City life.
She got a tutor for this homely man,
one beautiful but strictly one man's wife.
In Hammaborg the home is sacrosanct,
and entry is a rare and precious thing.
Frau Ermintrude sat Ordo down, enflanked
by children and her Einar, Herr, her king.
Submissive as she was at home, Prince Ord
would only see a straight, strong teacher's face.
She ran him through the course, his one reward
a smile each time he moved from gross to grace.
   He learned the dance as quickly as the rest;
   Miss Treudel Schlach became his final test.

Steel

We deem that iron has a mythic pow'r,
a metal that will neither melt nor flow.
It masters us; thus may it master our
worst nemeses, e'en those from hell below.
Consider now the Ulfbehrt sword, which was
but is no more. And can it come again
or is it, like to hell below, a fuzz
of thought which daylight hides from sight of men?
And what if Klarenz finds it out, to bake
a sword to match the former kind? What then
if Euwart sends Herr Schlach to firmly make
his status "permanently citizen?"
   Thus Ordo hides his fief 'neath subtle wing,
   and sets him up as tinker to the king.

Social Grace

What paragon of virtue do we see?
What master of his passions, free from flaw?
Yet here is Gnade, asking fair and free
for friendship straying well outside God's law.
Our prince has prayed and asked for help to bind
his heart, yet he's outplayed by just a child;
he thinks she lacks an educated mind,
mistaking mind for how she drives men wild.
She says that she's bespoke, but to a man
who's old and bent, and drinks himself to sleep.
So Ordo's mind becomes an also-ran
to hers, and Rigomonde calls him cheap.
   Anon miss Gnade plunders Ordo's poise;
    she counsels him, "Be quiet!" - then makes noise.

Sword

Two months of baking metal pies has taught
the fief to make pink metal that will chill
to bluish steel. His patient work has brought
forgotten craft to life, by wit and will.
With steel of every grade at ready hand
he builds a sword by layers so it's keen
of edge but yet the sword can flex, can stand
rough use; and do you see its mirror sheen?
Alike to Klarenz, Ordo studies men.
To read, to lead, to deal with those high-born
is self-taught too. One sees oneself, and then
one knows all manly vanity forsworn.
   Two students, two researchers, two achieve;
    poor Klarenz, though, must make his lord believe.

Social Disgrace

In public she assails him, and berates
Prince Ordowahl. He's treated her with cold
indifference, and thrown her to the Fates.
Where are his honor, love, once manifold?
The Lady Rigomonde comes to call
and ask him, does he see the wretched state
his thoughtless lust has caused – that plus the gall
to stand accused and then prevaricate?
His point of view is his, and when he shows
his mind she leaves. Then Euwart summons him,
to speak as prince to prince. Each of them knows
the other's mind, their peace an interim.
  Fief Klarenz saw it coming, yet stayed mum -
  hind-sights now with his Lord, ad nauseum.

Glittering Gifts

With rust and dirt and finest honing stone,
with careful finger down the slicing brim,
he made each razored mirror worth a throne,
full thirteen razored blades, bright gleaming, grim!
Unknowing, Ordowahl went out to test
his bondman's work. They hung a heavy beef
from sturdy oak; he brought a blade to rest
half-through a bovine spine and found belief.
Prince Euwart Four was next. When Klarenz made
the 'normal' sword go *thunk* 'twas fine; but when
Prince Euwart poised to swing a shiny blade
they coached him, "Euwart, gently stand, amen!"
  The curvy blade in Euwart's hands o'erdid:
  "Prince Nordland, stop! That damned blade I forbid!"

Winter Travel

Bad weather? There is none, just clothing that
does not suffice. Adrift in winter on
a southward trek, a three-day tent, a hat
of snow. They dream of May, wish winter gone.
"Has my fief heard of Blackish Knight?" "My liege,
I've not. Why ask of such?" "Much idle chat
arose on him; the weight of it laid siege,
starved out my skeptic mind; I dwell on that."
"My liege, you mentioned jackdaws from before;
are those that perch in yonder beech the same?"
"No, Klarenz, these are crows, in weather sore
for summer birds; is that Black Knight to blame?"
  They reach Ermsleben; it's Egeno's place.
  He finds them and invites with warm embrace.

Expectant Host

From winter camp to comfy house, both Ord
and Klarenz settle in. Their room is warm,
the horses safe, plus ample, simple board.
It isn't May, but let the winter storm!
And there's a price for peace like this; their host
Is anxious to discover what they hide.
It seems a moth had lost its wing, or most
of it: "Say why! – I beg you to confide."
What's more their host is anxious that no scandal
may erupt; "You must accept my tarts
into your beds. When you are known to dandle
one, you're less a risk to local hearts.
  Prince Ord depends on Klarenz to be wise:
  discretion with the swords, and with his eyes!

A Prince's Sword

Men-children play with shiny, girly strips
of steel, and little know the peril to
their necks. Prince Nordland has to come to grips
with them without creating much ado.
Of course Egeno's on the hunt. His wits
are keen and while he won't include his boys,
his guide, Black Knight, must gain the finer bits.
But Ordowahl stays mum and guards his poise.
So Klarenz beats two into one, invites
Egeno's sons, and works with pride. Its edge
and sheen are like to any other knight's,
and only Ord can sense the sacrilege.
    The weather warms; the jousting season starts.
    Egeno says, "Ord, Mind the Black Knight's arts."

The Black Knight

The prospect looms o'er vast and level field;
yet here is Klarenz, fall-down-drunk or sick.
The Black Knight comes, so smug; and he will yield
his henchman Heuermann, who'll do the trick.
But Klarenz reeks of Ingvik's acrid brew,
and Ordo tells him, calmly guard his wits.
Instead Ord has to worry now; his new
assistant and his health are opposites.
When Heuermann hands up the jousting lance
he oils its grip and takes the awkward side.
The Black Knight's second, seen in sidelong glance,
does likewise; how might these two coincide?
    It takes a mid-run shift to break the spell;
    the Knight hit hard, but 'twasn't Ord who fell.

The Black Knight's Power

Mid gathered throng a raven beaks the Knight,
laid crumpled on the ground, and up he stands.
"It seems, Prince Ord, you've knowledge recondite.
I've skill to trade with you; let's clasp our hands."
Ord knows to keep his friends to bosom bound,
and closer still his foes, e. g. this Knight
who now desires to joust another round -
"Please give a second chance, however slight."
"Friend Ord," Egeno warns, "Beware this Knight.
He's never lost like this; I fear his hand.
But also, friend, be sure to get this right;
To gain the Black Knight's trust is truly grand."
   Then Klarenz wakes, but under Black Knight's spell;
   To get him back, Ord nearly tolls his bell.

The Black Knight's Revenge

If less prepared; then more the loser he,
which took the precious hour to puzzle out:
what heat, what cold, what honey could that be
that signals death? The prince refused to doubt.
Reversing mail, he might upend the spell;
but what of horse, of shield, or lance? He went
and, blinded, held his lance, but still he fell;
his right arm useless, armor hot? Unspent!
The Black Knight's horse is gored; he sneering comes
and strikes at Ord, the armor at whose neck
deflects the blow. Left-armed, Ord pendulums
the Knight, whose own sword cancels raven's peck.
   Both flies and ravens swarm, then disappear;
   then Ordo heals, a jackdaw always near.

Hale and Farewell (Postlude)

"Tell how a Christian soul lies night by night
with one he's not betrothed, nor deems a wife?"
"Or husband either, Gelde. Is it right
to meld this stranger to your beddish life? "
The women that Egeno gave to Ord
and fief had more to them than simple flesh.
Although Egeno saw them only as a ward
'gainst towny talk, they taught their men afresh.
For yet another time Prince Ordowahl
had use, pro tem, of female company.
"In time, my dear, I'm sure you will enthrall
'her' if you spend this time in chat with me."
 And as all does, those soft days went to dust
 when Ordowahl returned to wanderlust.

On Poetry

Seven Pillars of Poetry

These are the seven attributes to look for in a poem; only the first four are necessary, but mastering all seven at once should be the glint in every poet's eye. In order of importance, best-first, these are the seven "pillars of poetry."

1 Strong emotional content
The emotion must be palpable, true to the human spirit, and made easily accessible through the words of the poem. A poem about a sunny day or a quiet moment will be a work of art when it splashes tanning, sweat-making sun onto your face, or stops you long enough to feel the deep peace of a truly quiet moment. Then it has "set up the pillar".

2 Powerful language
Diction, i.e. word choice, must go straight to the bone, yet also be both elegant and persuasive. It must be concise, unmistakable, and surprising. Ordinary homespun words of one syllable can do this; just choose them slowly, and well.

3 Powerful imagery
The poem should use simile and metaphor in ways that illustrate its feeling clearly, and persuasively. Suppose we take the rose as an image, or theme, or focus. "My love is like a red, red rose" is a simile. "My love has thorns; her deep red petals draw me in to embrace them" is a metaphor. Both evoke an image in the reader's mind.

The poet should aspire to set up and elaborate upon one consistent image throughout the poem.

4 Just like conversation
The poem should sound as though it were being spoken directly from the heart, with no inverted or twisted syntax, nothing overly cute or rhetorical except as required by e.g. a cute or rhetorical

speaker being quoted in context. Poems read in one's childhood may have tended to fall short of this, creating the impression that poetic speech is full of inverted syntax. When this thought creeps out of hiding, slay it.

5 Meter

If used, meter should be as tight as the stones of a dry-laid wall, yet not sing-songy. Sing-songy would be a brick wall with ab so lute ly rig id bricks, and all the joints mortared in. Meter should be reliable, yet incorporate occasional syllables that are neither stressed nor unstressed, but in between. In short, it should read like conversational, if somewhat elevated, language.

6 Rhyme

If used, the rhyming words should be chosen from the entire language, not just the one-syllable brace-rocks in that dry laid stone wall. Monosyllabics may be direct, blunt, and powerful; but the poet must use his or her whole vocabulary in all aspects of the poem, including rhyming words. Those rhyming words also need to be novel, surprising, powerful, ... (keep going)

The aa bb cc rhyme scheme works best when the line length is fairly long. So-called xaxa xbxb rhyme is in fact aa bb rhyme with long lines broken into halves.

Assonant or partial rhyme is like patchy frosting, something of a personal choice. My own preference is to eschew half-measures: if you include rhyme, then make it integral and strong.

Internal rhymes pop up inside a line according to no particular scheme. The effect of randomly placed internal rhymes, placed with apparent randomness, yet with care and attention, can be like the inner harmony of a Japanese rock garden.

7 Enjambment

enjambmnent ()n. The continuation of a syntactic unit from one line or couplet of a poem to the next with no pause.
In other words, the syntactic unit, such as a clause, phrase, etc., spills across a boundary because the line(s) just won't hold it.
Enjambment applies primarily to formal verse.

One citizen—one vote is fine; one thought—one line (OTOL) is not. Poems are made of many small smaller pieces, but not all of these will find proper expression in exactly one line. Enjambment is the successful divorce of The Line from The Thought.

What are the consequences of not using enjambment? The first, and worst, is that OTOL can trivialize a poem. If it won't fit on one line do you chuck it and use something simpler?—or is it that finding a notion that overflows the line is hard—it often is! Pump the iron, do the heavy lifting, until it's not hard any more.

A poem lacking enjambment pauses at the end of every line, which can impart its own 'sing-songy' effect. In the hands of a great master OTOL can work, but develop the mastery first.

TO BE (FORMAL) OR NOT TO BE (FORMAL)

There are two primary schools in modern poetry. Over the past half-century poets have increasingly relegated classic poetry to a formalistic past. Ostensibly form interferes with one's ability to let the spirit speak. Only a few words fit any given rhyme, hence formalisms such as rhyme restrict the poet's choice of words. Does the restriction stifle the voice?—or does it simply make writing good verse harder? Each school has its own answer.

When rhyming disappears but meter remains, the result is "blank verse." Whole plays used to be written that way. Not just The Bard but his contemporaries all used blank verse, such as iambic pentameter.

When meter disappears as well the result is "free verse." With only four pillars to rely on, not seven, good free verse is actually harder to write well.

In fact new formalisms continue to pop up, such as 'shape' or 'concrete' poems, syllable-counting forms such as haiku, rictameter, and so on. It appears that some poets need new formalisms to replace the discarded set.

Poets who still embrace formalism remind us that Shakespeare used formalism as less a crutch than a framework, a trellis on which to grow marvelously expressive works. Modern formalists employ a richly evolved vocabulary to reinvigorate classical forms or more generally any rhymed and metered verse.

A breathtakingly beautiful poem does not require rhyme and/or meter. In fact any poem should be breathtakingly beautiful, compressed, concise, expressive, eloquent and flow naturally, or it shouldn't merit the name. A mythical WORLD'S GREATEST POEM might perfect all seven Pillars, with none higher than any other, i.e. all at the limits of human perfection, but the proof is in the cake, not the icing.

Backing away from that ideal by omitting one or more of these seven requires the poet to polish those that remain.

"Free" verse is anything but. Freedom always comes at a price. A poet writing free verse must go beyond expressing a thought or feeling; prose is capable of *piercing* expressiveness. Free verse must do so in a breathtaking way, and this requires both inspiration and hard-earned craft. To offer as "poetry" something that took no time or effort to write and received no subsequent polish, is to offend the art.

DENSE, ELEGANT, POWERFUL LANGUAGE

The best language does not always consist of the longest possible words. Instead it may often compress complex thoughts into simple words. Characterizing "the best language" is akin to herding cats, or nailing jello to the wall. When you write something that sounds powerful and you're still proud of it on the fifth or eighth reading, you may have used "the best language."

MARKING METER

How do you visualize a verse's metrical construction? Here is one method, among many:

Beneath each line of a poem place a separate line with one mark per syllable. Use '1' for a stressed syllable, '-' for an unstressed syllable, and 'i' for a syllable that won't go quietly into either camp. Using these marks will illustrate what kind of 'foot' is in use, and whether all feet are from the animal.

Metrical poetry uses five kinds of feet:

noun	adjective	marks	effect	example
spondee	spondylic	1	stomp	
iamb	iambic	-1	moonwalk	i AM
trochee	trochaic	1-	stride	TROchee
anapest	anapestic	--1	hoppy moonwalk	an a PEST
dactyl	dactylic	1--	hoppy stride	DAC tyl ic

Iambic is the most common. In Shakespeare's time all plays tended to be written in iambic pentameter, i.e. five iambs per line:

I am a quiet diplomat of peace
-1-1-1-1-1
Who nonetheless surmounts e'er war of man
-1-1-1-1-1
Or earthly beast might God's good Will release
-1-1-1-1-1
Upon the land or ocean—none began
-1-1-1-1-1
But ended soon by this my weapon'd arm.
-1-1-1-1-1

You get the point. Now, think of the '1' as the heel; every foot has one. The '-' syllables are like toes, and the foot either stomps (spondee), strides forward (trochee or dactyl) or does a moonwalk (iamb or anapest).

\

METER IMPACTING RHYME

Not all lines have to be exact; a formalist may sometimes fudge the unaccented syllable at either end of a line, usually by leaving it off. When there is an extra '-' on the end of an iambic line, one might omit the '-' at the start of the next line so the flow doesn't falter. Changes like this should not leave the rhyme on a different stress. For example, one line has an extra syllable, the next line has one too few, but the ryhyme and meter don't suffer:

My name is never Pete; I never am deceitful
-1-1-1-1-1-1-
But whene'er we greet upon the street I'm Pete!
 1-1-1-1-1-1-1

When a poem's meter is in trouble, i.e. when it wears different shoes from foot to foot or it wants to have different numbers of feet per line, what do you do?

You write the notion(s) in those line(s) in as many ways as you can think of, then write them several other ways, until you get just the right reading. This is like pumping iron: the more work goes in, the more powerful the results that eventually come out. Your metrical muscles may take over, to the point that you may stop yourself and realize you've been writing in iambics in the middle of some intense passage in a private letter.

Rule One when resolving a meter or rhyme issue: **rewrite** but start with eyes closed—picture a blank wall in your mind, and let the words come out and play with each other. Some adventurous phrase will eventually reach up and rap at the inside of an eyelid, your eyes will fly open, and your fingers will release it onto the screen.

Rule Two: if you are painted into a corner, go back to find whatever it was that put you there, and **rewrite THAT**.

FINDING RHYME

Enjambment deserves mention here. One of the hallmarks of the minor leagues of poetry is to use rhyme but then to trivialize its expression via the "one thought—one line" (OTOL) rubric. Looking for places to enjamb counters that.

When using rhyme, to quote Yoda,

There is no try; there is only do or do not.

If you very delicately use near rhyme, keep a light touch. But if you are going to follow a rhyme scheme, for poetry's sake please consider the following carefully.

Good and Bad Rhyme Schemes

First, the use of 'x' in a rhyme scheme, usually xaxa xbxb ..., can be a misnomer; xaxa is really aa where you've broken each long line in the middle; regard this as whole long lines. Since FanStory's format for poetry is a narrow window, long lines come out broken anyway. You can post it as prose and say in a note that it's really "long line poetry" but that's not going to do you any good in a poetry contest, is it? So go head and write it xaxa xbxb, and put a suitable grumble in the Author Notes to the effect that it's really aa bb.

If you have some other use for x, e.g. abxab bcxbc ... then bravo, go right ahead. Just tell your readers what the format is. The more formats you become familiar with, or known for (or invent),the more polished a poet you are likely to become.

Second, rhymed couplets of aa bb ... are like class A baseball in that you advance to class AA, then AAA, and then the Major Leagues. Your skills will be there to see, but the aa bb rhyme scheme tends to drag the poet into simplistic, unpoetic thoughts. Or it may be the other way 'round: a poet with undeveloped skills is often only able to visualize rhymes in couplets. It's your choice, but if you work in couplets it may create a shallow impression.

The next step up, and a personal favorite, is abab cdcd ... This doesn't tax the reader as much as for instance abba cddc ..., which uses a rhymed couplet in the middle, for the even-numbered rhymes, and sticks the odd-numbered rhymes at some distance from each other.

Another challenging scheme is aa..aa bb..bb, i.e. each verse, of whatever length, uses the same rhyme. War Story Alert: in college a friend of mine composed something with every line ending in 'ation'. Well, there are a ton of those, so there was no challenge in that. Your humble and obedient servant found a rhyming dictionary and selected "ection", of which there perhaps twenty-six, and composed a reply using them *in alphabetical order*. The result was half doggerel and half gibberish. :) There is a clear lesson in there, somewhere, regarding whether you will master a rhyme scheme, or it will master you.

Third, and of great importance to the elegance, beauty, and power of your poem, is to freely use multi-syllable words. Of course one syllable rhyming words are the easiest to aim at. You start at the front of the line and write toward any of the dozens of one syllable words which may fit your rhyme scheme; you'll even find that you've done this for the *first* rhyme!

But staking that one-syllable rhyming word out there does several things to your result, all of them bad. First, it may keep you from enjambing. Second, it limits your vocabulary; how powerfully can you write when you can only use a simple monosyllable at the end of each line? Third, it seems to encourage contorted syntax, since lots of those words tend to be parts of speech that DON'T come at the end of a natural phrase or sentence, yet there you are, putting them at the end of your phrase/line/sentence.

OK, longer words can also wind up "requiring" contorted syntax; please don't surrender to this idea. If syntax is suffering, stop and start over. Put a good rhyming word out there at the end of your unwritten line, then write toward it WITH PROPER SYNTAX.

Fourth is something called "half-rhyme", i.e. pairs of words that are near misses. Here are some: made—plaid, make—breaks, thing—thin—you get the picture. If you're going to use near-rhyme throughout a poem, fine. But if you're going to establish an actual rhyme scheme, then near-rhyme is acceptable very occasionally. Think of it as a "beauty mark". Do you remember seeing old pictures of Marilyn Monroe? She had a very creamy complexion, and would put a tiny black dot somewhere low on one cheek where its imperfection would highlight the smooth perfection of the rest of her face.

MORE ON ERECTING PILLARS

Consider any poem, formal or not, disguised by being collapsed into one or a few paragraphs. Such a thing is an ideal starting point for formal verse, for that matter—why start with a lesser thing?

Imagine following these simple steps:

A have something to say, express, define, explain, . . .
B express it in your personal best free verse poem
IF FORMAL:
 C reformat the raw text into one or more paragraphs, i.e. get rid of all the line breaks
 D rewrite it, as gently as possible, into metered, rhymed verse

So how does one evaluate the result of whichever final step. We'll stipulate that the poet understands a good step B when (s)he sees one; but how can you tell when you're done?

Here's one way:

Reformat it back into one or more paragraphs by getting rid of all the line breaks.

Now, does it scan as something the nightly news anchor could read on camera, as prose?—elegantly? Not because it was your own prose, but because in addition to being very grammatically regular, correct, unexceptional prose it was also the sort of thing you'd judge to be good free verse. And if formal, it has he right physical aspects, such as syllable count or a subtle but regular underlying beat, maybe rhymes pop up at regular intervals.

Every word would be in the exact place it would occupy in regular prose.

Every rhyme would also be a word that fits the meaning and syntax of the text.

Other than the regular meter and periodic rhyming, would it meet the "nightly news" criterion?

THAT [[again, personal opinion]] is good verse.

Returning to the question of how one brings what's on the page ever closer to "ideal", do this: put the text back into paragraph form one more time. Read it closely; make a mark everywhere it falls short.

With a page full of marks, go back and use the generic techniques for rewriting, and edit the poem.

Repeat the foregoing, i.e. rewrite verse, collapse back to paragraph form and edit for value, until there is some stopping condition:
- The verge of exhaustion
- Completely out of ideas
- Looking madly through the computer's manual for its "Halt and Catch Fire" machine instruction
- Dinner is served

Set the poem aside. When tomorrow comes, either post it, or repeat the above exercise. Or both.

Paul Valery, French literary figure who died in 1945, is best remembered for saying that "No poem is ever finished, merely abandoned." Stephen King says of fiction, "Murder your darlings," said darlings being chapters, plot points, pages, characters – never be afraid of some hearty triage. Same for poems: if you can't improve on it, let it be. It may even live.

Glass half-empty: WOE IS ME!

Glass half-full: Go ahead and post: my so-far-best will have to do.

9 780997 032642